SOCIAL SKILLS FOR TEENS

9 ESSENTIAL STEPS TO A NEW SOCIAL LIFE, BUILDING TRUE BONDS, AND FOSTERING RESILIENCE AND PERSONAL GROWTH

ALEXANDER KNIGHT

CONTENTS

Introduction	7
CHAPTER 1	11
The Mirror Exercise: Seeing Yourself Clearly	11
Your Emotional Spectrum: Identifying Feelings	13
Self-Esteem Builders: Practices to Boost Confidence	16
Overcoming the Fear of Judgment	18
The Power of Positive Self-Talk	21
CHAPTER 2: NAVIGATING THE DIGITAL SELF	25
Crafting Your Digital Persona: The Dos and Don'ts	25
Social Media Etiquette: Respecting Boundaries	28
Cyberbullying: Understanding and Combatting	30
Digital Detox: Finding the Right Balance	32
Privacy and Safety Online: What Teens Need to Know	35
CHAPTER 3: THE ART OF CONVERSATION	39
Conversation Starters: Beyond "Hi"	39
Reading the Room: When to Speak and When to Listen	42
Small Talk, Big Impact: Finding Common Ground	44
The Follow-Up: Keeping the Conversation Going	46
Exiting Conversations Gracefully	48
CHAPTER 4: CULTIVATING CONNECTIONS	53
Making New Friends: Strategies That Work	53
The Art of Empathy: Understanding Others	56
Conflict Resolution: Navigating Disagreements	59
Keeping Connections Strong: Friendship Maintenance	62
Dealing With Toxic Relationships	64
CHAPTER 5: BREATHING LIFE INTO SOCIAL CONFIDENCE	69
Breathing Techniques for Anxiety Control	69
Visualization for Social Confidence	72

Managing Rejection: It's Not About You	74
Stepping Out of Your Comfort Zone Safely	77
From Shy to Sociable: A Gradual Transformation	79

CHAPTER 6: NAVIGATING PEER INFLUENCE	85
Understanding Peer Pressure: The Why Behind It	85
Saying "No" with Confidence	87
Strategies to Counteract Bullying	90
Building a Support System	92
Empowering Yourself in the Face of Adversity	95

CHAPTER 7: DIGITAL COMMUNICATION MASTERY	99
Texting Etiquette: Dos and Don'ts	99
Social Media: Connecting Responsibly	102
Handling Online Misunderstandings	104
The Role of Video Calls in Maintaining Relationships	107
Online Gaming: Social Skills in Virtual Spaces	110

CHAPTER 8: PREPARING FOR LIFE'S MILESTONES	113
The First Job Interview: Making a Good Impression	113
College Interviews: Showcasing Your Social Savvy	115
Dating: Respectful and Healthy Approaches	118
Navigating Family Gatherings	120
Moving to a New School or City	123

CHAPTER 9: BUILDING A PERSONAL BLUEPRINT FOR SOCIAL SUCCESS	127
Setting Social Goals: Short and Long Term	127
Tracking Progress: Tools and Techniques	130
Learning from Failure: Resilience in Practice	132
Seeking Feedback: The Role of Mentors and Peers	135
Celebrating Successes: Recognizing Your Growth	138

CHAPTER 10: SUPPORTING THE SOCIAL EXPLORER	143
The Crucial Role of Parents and Educators	
How Parents Can Support Without Overstepping	144
Educators as Social Skill Coaches	146
Creating Environments That Foster Social Skills	148

Conclusion 153
References 157

INTRODUCTION

During a bustling school lunch hour, amidst the cacophony of clattering trays and boisterous conversations, one teen finds themselves frozen at the threshold of the cafeteria. Anxiety grips them as they scan the room for a familiar face, a safe harbor in this sea of judgment and expectation. This moment, fraught with the fear of rejection and misunderstanding, is one that echoes in the hearts of many teens navigating the complex world of socialization. It is from this very scene of everyday struggle that our journey begins.

This book is born out of a profound desire to empower you, the teen reader, with the foundational social skills necessary for building meaningful connections, fostering resilience, and nurturing personal growth. Through a combination of actionable advice, scenarios drawn from real life, and engaging interactive exercises, we will tackle the unique challenges you face in today's digital age. From navigating the nuanced dynamics of online communication to building self-esteem away from the keyboard, our exploration will be both broad and deeply personal.

What sets this guide apart is its commitment to addressing the modern dilemmas of digital communication and social media, while grounding our discussions in the wisdom of psychological expertise and a decade-long experience in youth mentorship. My name is Alexander Knight, and my journey through psychology and mentoring young individuals like yourself has equipped me with insights into the social landscapes you navigate daily. This book distills those insights into relatable, actionable guidance designed to resonate with a wide array of experiences and challenges.

Inclusivity is at the heart of our mission. This book is crafted to ensure that every teen, regardless of their background or the nature of their social dilemmas, finds relevance and support in these pages. We steer clear of one-size-fits-all solutions and stereotypes, focusing instead on fostering a sense of self-esteem and personal growth that celebrates the diversity of teen experiences.

As you turn these pages, expect to find a rich blend of theoretical insights, compelling real-life examples, practical tools, and interactive elements that will not only engage but also equip you to navigate your social world with newfound confidence and resilience. A curated list of resources for further exploration underscores our commitment to your ongoing journey of personal and social development.

I invite you to approach this book with an open mind and a willingness to dive into the exercises and strategies we've laid out. Consider this the first step toward a transformed social life, marked by deeper connections and a stronger sense of self.

Let this book be your guide as you embark on this journey, not just towards improved social skills, but towards realizing the potential for growth and fulfillment that lies within each of you. Remember, the path to a richer, more connected life is paved with the courage to be vulnerable, the strength to be authentic, and the wisdom to listen and learn. Together, let's turn the page on social anxiety and isolation, towards a future brimming with true bonds and endless possibilities for personal growth.

CHAPTER 1

In the quiet solace of the morning, when the world still slumbers in its gentle embrace of tranquility, a solitary figure stands before a mirror. This act, simplistic in its execution, is profound in its implications. It is a moment of confrontation and introspection, a silent dialogue between the self and the reflection that stares back. This daily ritual, often overlooked in its ordinariness, holds the key to unlocking a deeper understanding of oneself, serving as the bedrock upon which the edifice of social skills is built. The mirror, in its unyielding honesty, reflects more than just the contours of a face; it reveals the contours of the soul, laying bare the emotions and insecurities that writhe beneath the surface.

THE MIRROR EXERCISE: SEEING YOURSELF CLEARLY

Introspection through Reflection

The act of standing before a mirror is not merely an exercise in vanity but a practice in mindfulness and self-awareness. It compels one to confront the visage that confronts the world. As you gaze into your own eyes, questions begin to surface, whispers of thoughts that often go unheeded in the cacophony of daily life. What emotions do you see mirrored in those eyes? Is it confidence that shines forth, or do you find shadows of doubt lurking in their depths? This moment of reflection is a call to introspection, an invitation to delve into the self and explore the emotions that rise to the surface. It encourages you to question why certain feelings emerge in response to your own reflection and what they reveal about your inner state.

Self-Acceptance

The journey to self-acceptance begins with acknowledging what the mirror reflects back. It requires the courage to embrace every aspect of your appearance and the emotions that accompany it. This acceptance is the foundation upon which self-confidence is built. It is a recognition that your worth is not contingent upon external approval but is inherent in your being. By accepting yourself, you affirm your value, setting the stage for growth and development. Self-acceptance liberates you from the shackles of self-doubt, allowing you to present yourself to the world with assurance and grace.

Non-Verbal Cues

The mirror is a silent teacher, instructing you in the language of non-verbal cues. As you observe your reflection, pay attention to the nuances of your facial expressions. These subtle shifts convey volumes, speaking a language without words. They are the emissaries of your emotions, conveying your feelings to those around you. By becoming aware of these non-verbal cues, you learn to control the narrative that your face tells. You begin to understand how a furrowed brow might be interpreted as worry or how a smile, even a tentative one, can be a bridge to connection.

This awareness is instrumental in social interactions, where nonverbal cues often speak louder than words.

Building a Positive Self-Image

The mirror exercise is not merely an act of observation but a proactive tool for sculpting a positive self-image. Each day, as you stand before the mirror, challenge yourself to find one aspect of your reflection that you appreciate. It could be the curve of your smile, the intensity of your gaze, or the resilience that your posture suggests. This practice of positive reinforcement serves to gradually construct a self-image grounded in appreciation and respect for oneself. Over time, this nurtured self-image becomes a wellspring of confidence, empowering you to navigate social settings with ease and assurance.

In essence, the mirror exercise is a ritual of self-discovery and affirmation. It teaches you to see yourself clearly, to accept yourself unconditionally, and to communicate with the world not just through words, but through the silent language of self-assurance. Through this daily practice, you lay the cornerstone of a robust social foundation, one that supports not only the development of advanced social skills but also the cultivation of a resilient and positive self-identity.

YOUR EMOTIONAL SPECTRUM: IDENTIFYING FEELINGS

In the kaleidoscope of human experience, emotions paint our days with the hues of joy, sadness, anger, and love, each shade as vital as the next in the grand tapestry of life. This rich emotional palette, while beautiful in its diversity, can often be overwhelming, leaving one to navigate a labyrinth of feelings without a map. The quest for emotional literacy, then, becomes not just an academic endeavor, but a crucial skill in understanding the self and enhancing interactions with the world.

The first step in this quest is the identification and naming of emotions, a task that might seem rudimentary yet is anything but. For many, emotions are felt viscerally, experienced as a physical sensation before they are understood cognitively. The fluttering of anxiety in the stomach, the warmth of joy spreading through the chest, the prickly heat of anger — these sensations precede the naming of the emotion, acting as the body's signal flare. To name an emotion is to acknowledge its presence, to bring it into the light of consciousness where it can be examined and understood. This act of naming is empowering, providing a lexicon for the soul that enriches one's emotional intelligence.

Yet, emotions do not arise in a vacuum. They are triggered by events, interactions, and memories, each acting as a catalyst in the alchemy of feeling. To map one's emotional landscape, it is crucial to trace these emotions back to their source, to understand the why behind the what. This exploration reveals patterns, shedding light on how certain situations or interactions serve as consistent triggers for specific emotions. For instance, the anxiety that bubbles up before a public speaking engagement or the irritation that flares when faced with unwarranted criticism. Recognizing these triggers is akin to identifying the wires in a complex circuitry, allowing for a more nuanced control over one's emotional responses.

This control hinges on the crucial distinction between feeling an emotion and reacting to it. Emotions, in their raw form, are uncontrollable; they surge forth unbidden, a primal response to the world. However, the reaction to these emotions is a matter of choice. It is the space between stimulus and response where power lies, the moment of decision where one can choose to be swept away by the current of emotion or to navigate the waters with intention. This differentiation is subtle yet profound, offering a measure of control in the often turbulent seas of human experience. It is not about suppressing emotions but about responding to them in a way that is aligned with one's values and goals.

The tool that facilitates this nuanced understanding of emotions and their triggers is the humble journal. Encouraging the practice of keeping a journal serves multiple purposes: it acts as a container for emotions, a space where they can be expressed freely without judgment; it serves as a mirror, reflecting the patterns and triggers of one's emotional responses; and it functions as a guide, offering insights into the self that might have remained obscured. The act of writing, of translating emotions into words, requires a level of reflection that deepens one's understanding of these emotions. It prompts questions: Why did this event trigger such a strong reaction? What does this emotion say about my needs or desires? How can I respond to this emotion in a way that serves me better?

Through this practice, the journal becomes more than just a collection of entries; it becomes a map of one's emotional terrain, a tool for navigation and self-discovery. It allows for the tracking of progress, the recognition of patterns, and the formulation of strategies for managing emotions and their triggers. This process of journaling, then, is not just an exercise in writing but an act of self-care, a deliberate and intentional approach to understanding and managing one's emotional world.

In this endeavor, the rewards are manifold. With increased emotional literacy comes a deeper connection to the self, a heightened empathy for others, and an enhanced capability for navigating the complexities of human relationships. It fosters a resilience that is rooted in understanding, allowing one to face the vicissitudes of life with a grounded sense of self. This journey through the emotional spectrum, with its challenges and revelations, is not just about managing emotions but about enriching the very fabric of one's experience. It is about painting one's days with a broader palette, embracing the full range of human emotion with understanding, compassion, and grace.

SELF-ESTEEM BUILDERS: PRACTICES TO BOOST CONFIDENCE

In the realm of personal growth, the cultivation of self-esteem stands as a beacon, illuminating the path toward a fulfilling and authentic social life. This elusive quarry, often buried beneath layers of self-doubt and societal expectation, demands a nuanced approach to its unearthing. Among the most potent tools in this endeavor are the practices of positive affirmations, goal setting, the cultivation of supportive relationships, and the celebration of one's uniqueness. Each practice, like the notes in a complex melody, harmonizes to elevate the individual's sense of self-worth and confidence.

Positive affirmations serve as the first note in this symphony, a subtle yet powerful incantation against the specter of negative self-talk. These affirmations, simple statements of self-worth and capability, act as a counterbalance to the often critical internal dialogue that erodes confidence. The practice of repeating these affirmations daily, with conviction and sincerity, embeds them into the subconscious, gradually altering the internal narrative. Over time, the mind begins to accept these positive statements as truth, a mental alchemy transforming doubt into belief. Yet, the efficacy of affirmations lies not in their repetition alone but in their believability and relevance. Crafting affirmations that resonate with the individual's aspirations and challenges ensures they strike a chord, reverberating through the psyche and fostering a growing sense of self-assurance.

Parallel to the practice of affirmations is the setting of achievable goals. This process, grounded in the tangible, provides a roadmap for personal progress, each milestone a testament to the individual's capability and determination. Small, realistic goals serve as stepping stones, building a sense of accomplishment and self-worth with each achievement. The key lies in their specificity and attainability; goals set too high risk the precipice of failure and the erosion of confidence. Yet, when calibrated to the individual's current abilities, with an eye toward gradual expansion, these goals become a source of motivation and a mirror reflecting the individual's growing competence. This practice of goal setting, therefore, becomes not just a pursuit of external achievement but a ritual of self-validation, each accomplishment reinforcing the individual's belief in their own potential.

The environment in which an individual chooses to immerse themselves plays a critical role in the nurturing of self-esteem. Surrounding oneself with positivity, be it through relationships that uplift and support or environments that inspire and energize, acts as a buffer against the slings and arrows of everyday challenges. The company one keeps can either feed the flames of self-doubt or fan the embers of self-assurance. Therefore, the deliberate selection of friends and spaces that resonate with positivity and encouragement is crucial. These relationships and environments serve as a mirror, reflecting back the individual's worth and potential, reinforcing their self-esteem. The act of choosing positivity is, in itself, an affirmation of the individual's worth, a declaration that they deserve to be uplifted and supported.

At the heart of self-esteem lies the celebration of one's uniqueness, an acknowledgment of the individual's inherent value and the diverse tapestry of traits that distinguish them. This celebration is an act of defiance against the homogenizing pressures of society, a reclaiming of the self in all its idiosyncratic glory. Embracing and highlighting personal strengths and unique qualities challenge the notion of worth being tethered to conformity. It fosters a sense of pride and self-acceptance, crucial components of self-esteem. This celebration is not a one-time event but a continuous practice, a lens through which the individual views themselves and navigates the world. It requires mindfulness, the ability to recognize and appreciate the nuances of one's character and abilities. In this way, the celebration of uniqueness becomes a wellspring of confidence, a constant reminder of the individual's irreplaceable contribution to the world around them.

In their confluence, these practices—affirmations, goal setting, surrounding oneself with positivity, and celebrating uniqueness—forge a robust foundation for self-esteem. They intertwine, each reinforcing and amplifying the other, to create a holistic approach to the cultivation of confidence. This process is not linear but cyclical, each iteration deepening the individual's sense of self-worth and their capacity for authentic social engagement. Through this ongoing practice, self-esteem is not merely constructed but continually nurtured, evolving in tandem with the individual's growth. It becomes a touchstone, a source of strength and resilience in the face of life's vicissitudes, empowering the individual to navigate their social world with assurance and grace.

OVERCOMING THE FEAR OF JUDGMENT

The specter of judgment lurks in the shadows of social interactions, a silent arbiter of actions and words, casting a long shadow over the landscape of human connection. This pervasive fear, deeply ingrained in the fabric of our psyche, often finds its roots in the fertile ground of our earliest social experiences. From the tender years of childhood, where the playground becomes a crucible for acceptance and rejection, to the tumultuous seas of adolescence, where every glance and whisper is magnified, the fear of being judged is cultivated. It thrives on the human craving for belonging and acceptance, feeding on the dread of ostracization and the sting of ridicule.

In confronting this fear, the first step lies in disentangling the intricate web of thoughts and emotions that it weaves. It demands an exploration into the genesis of this fear, tracing its tendrils back to moments of vulnerability when the desire for acceptance was met with the cold hand of rejection. This journey into the self is not a simple excavation of past hurts but a nuanced understanding of how these experiences shape the perception of social landscapes. It reveals how the fear of judgment clouds judgment itself, distorting the reality of interactions and erecting barriers where none exist.

Rationalizing these fears becomes a crucial strategy in diminishing their power. It involves a meticulous process of questioning the validity of the fear in the present context. Is the fear of judgment rooted in reality, or is it a ghost from the past haunting the present? This questioning is not a denial of the fear but a critical examination of its relevance and accuracy. Rationalization serves as a balm, soothing the raw edges of fear with the salve of logic and reason. It provides a perspective that places judgment in its proper place, not as a looming threat but as one of many facets of social interaction, no more significant than the myriad of positive outcomes possible.

The arena of social experimentation offers a controlled setting to test the waters of interaction, dipping one's toes into the social currents with the safety of knowing the shore is within reach. These experiments, small in scale but significant in impact, serve as a proving ground for new behaviors and responses. Perhaps it begins with a smile offered to a stranger, an opinion shared in a group setting, or a compliment extended without expectation. Each act, though seemingly inconsequential, is a step towards desensitization, a gradual reduction in the sensitivity to judgment. With each positive outcome, the fear of judgment recedes, its hold weakened by evidence of acceptance and connection. These experiments are not about seeking validation from others but about validating one's capacity to engage in social interactions without being paralyzed by fear.

Amidst this personal exploration and experimentation, the role of peer support emerges as a beacon of reassurance. Sharing one's fears with trusted friends or family is akin to bringing a wound to light. It allows for the cleansing air of understanding and empathy to touch the rawness of fear, initiating the healing process. This act of vulnerability, far from being a sign of weakness, is a testament to strength. It acknowledges the universal nature of the fear of judgment, fostering a sense of solidarity and shared humanity. Peer support offers not just comfort but a mirror reflecting the distorted perceptions fueled by fear. Through the eyes of trusted others, the fear of judgment is seen for what it often is - an inflated specter, devoid of the power it wields in the shadows of the mind.

In this collective and individual endeavor to transcend the fear of judgment, the journey itself transforms. It becomes not just a path towards diminishing a specific fear but a broader exploration of self-awareness, resilience, and the capacity for genuine connection. The fear of judgment, once a formidable barrier, becomes a stepping stone, a catalyst for growth that propels one towards richer, more authentic social interactions.

THE POWER OF POSITIVE SELF-TALK

Within the confines of our minds, a ceaseless dialogue unfolds, a narrative that shapes our perception of self and our interactions with the world. This internal monologue, often unnoticed, wields significant influence, capable of elevating spirits or casting shadows over our confidence. Recognizing the patterns of this self-talk, therefore, becomes a task of paramount importance, a step towards reclaiming the narrative that guides our lives.

Negative self-talk, with its insidious whispers of doubt and criticism, often finds its roots in past experiences and societal expectations. It is a familiar voice, one that echoes our deepest insecurities and fears, painting our efforts and aspirations with the brush of inadequacy. The task of identifying these negative patterns demands vigilance, an attuned awareness to the moments when our internal dialogue turns against us, undermining our confidence and distorting our view of our capabilities. It is in these moments, at the precipice of self-doubt, that the opportunity for transformation lies.

Replacing the cacophony of negativity with the harmonious notes of positivity is akin to learning a new language, one that speaks of potential, resilience, and worth. This shift begins with the conscious choice to interrupt the flow of critical thoughts, to pause and question their validity. It is a process of disentanglement, of separating the self from the barrage of negativity that seeks to define it. Techniques such as reframing thoughts, where negative statements are turned on their head to reveal a positive aspect, or the use of positive affirmations that affirm one's worth and capabilities, become tools in this endeavor.

These methods are not mere platitudes but acts of defiance against the tide of self-criticism, a reclamation of the narrative that shapes our self-perception.

The role of self-talk in building confidence cannot be overstated. It is the bedrock upon which our sense of self is built, influencing not only how we view ourselves but how we engage with others. Positive self-talk, with its affirmations of worth and capability, fosters a self-image that is resilient and empowered. It colors our interactions with the world with the hues of confidence, enabling us to navigate social landscapes with ease and assurance. This shift in internal dialogue is transformative, altering not only how we perceive challenges but how we approach them. Where once there was hesitation, now there is readiness; where doubt once took root, now conviction stands.

Mindfulness, the practice of staying present and engaged with the current moment, offers a pathway to cultivating a positive internal dialogue. It is an exercise in focused attention, a deliberate act of tuning into the now, where the narratives of past failures and future anxieties hold no sway. Through mindfulness, we become observers of our thoughts and feelings, acknowledging their presence without allowing them to define our self-worth. Techniques such as focused breathing, where attention is anchored to the rhythm of breath, or body scans, where awareness is systematically directed through different parts of the body, serve to ground us in the present. This centeredness affords us a clarity of perspective, a vantage point from which the din of negative self-talk fades into the background, leaving space for a dialogue of compassion and self-acceptance.

As we navigate the ebb and flow of daily life, armed with the tools of positive self-talk and mindfulness, we find ourselves less swayed by the currents of doubt and criticism. This steady cultivation of a positive internal dialogue is not a destination but a continuous journey, one that unfolds with each moment of awareness and choice. It is a path marked by growth, resilience, and an ever-deepening understanding of the self. In this space of self-awareness and acceptance, we discover the freedom to engage with the world with openness, confidence, and a profound sense of our own worth.

CHAPTER 2: NAVIGATING THE DIGITAL SELF

In a world where the digital and physical realms intertwine like the strands of a DNA helix, our online personas have become as integral to our identities as the clothes we wear or the languages we speak. Here, amidst the glow of screens and the endless scroll of social feeds, we craft versions of ourselves that traverse the globe in seconds, leaving digital footprints in the sands of the vast internet. This digital self, an avatar of pixels and text, carries with it the weight of our reputations, aspirations, and, most importantly, our authenticity. It's a realm where the line between reality and virtuality blurs, demanding not just our attention but a keen sense of responsibility and self-awareness.

CRAFTING YOUR DIGITAL PERSONA: THE DOS AND DON'TS

Authenticity Online

The digital world, much like a grand masquerade, tempts us with the allure of crafting personas that may stray far from our true selves. Yet, the mask of anonymity and the facade of perfection can often lead to a chasm between who we are and what we portray. Consider the Instagram feed, meticulously curated to showcase a flawless life of adventure, success, and happiness, each post a brushstroke in a portrait of idealized existence. This disparity, while seemingly benign, carries the risk of eroding our sense of self, leaving us stranded in the pursuit of an unattainable digital image. Authenticity online, then, becomes a beacon, guiding us back to our genuine selves, ensuring our digital persona reflects our true values, beliefs, and character. It's about embracing imperfections, sharing genuine moments, and connecting with others in a way that transcends the superficial, fostering deeper, more meaningful interactions.

Privacy Settings and Information Sharing

In the labyrinth of social media settings and privacy policies, navigating the complexities of what to share, with whom, and how, poses a challenge that demands vigilance. The act of adjusting privacy settings, often overlooked in the rush to connect and share, is akin to setting the boundaries of our digital homes, determining who gets a key and who remains a visitor. It's about making informed choices, understanding the implications of sharing personal information, locations, and moments. The guiding principle here is discretion, a measured approach to sharing that protects not only our privacy but the sanctity of our personal lives.

The Impact on Real-Life Relationships

The ripple effect of our online behavior on real-life relationships is a phenomenon observed with growing frequency and concern. A tweet, a status update, or a shared photo, seemingly inconsequential in the digital ether, can have tangible effects on friendships, family ties, and professional connections. It's a reminder that behind every profile, like, and comment, lies a real person, with emotions, expectations, and a relationship to us that extends beyond the screen. Thus, digital mindfulness becomes imperative, a conscious effort to ensure that our online actions enrich, rather than erode, our real-world relationships.

Consistency Across Platforms

In the digital mosaic of social media platforms, each piece, from LinkedIn to TikTok, contributes to the overarching picture of our digital persona. Consistency in this context does not imply uniformity but rather a coherent narrative that threads through our various online presences. It's the recognition that, whether we're sharing professional accomplishments on LinkedIn, creative expressions on Instagram, or personal milestones on Facebook, each post is a chapter of the same story. This coherence not only aids in maintaining the integrity of our digital self but also in building a recognizable and relatable persona across the digital spectrum.

Visual Element: Crafting Your Digital Persona Checklist

To navigate the creation and maintenance of your digital persona, consider this checklist as a compass:

1. **Authenticity Check**: Before posting, ask if this content reflects your true self and values.
2. **Privacy Audit**: Regularly review privacy settings and the information you've shared online.
3. **Impact Analysis**: Consider how your online actions might affect your real-life relationships.
4. **Consistency Review**: Ensure your digital narratives across platforms tell a coherent story about you.
5. **Engagement Evaluation**: Engage with others online in a way that fosters positive interactions and connections.

By following these guidelines, you can navigate the digital world with confidence, crafting a digital persona that not only resonates with authenticity but also enhances your real-world interactions and relationships.

SOCIAL MEDIA ETIQUETTE: RESPECTING BOUNDARIES

In the sprawling expanse of the digital domain, the concept of boundaries becomes both abstract and absolutely crucial. Navigating these invisible lines requires not just an understanding of one's own comfort zones but also a respect for the limits of others. It is akin to moving through a crowded room, where personal space is negotiated through subtle cues and mutual respect. Online, however, these cues become obscured by screens, demanding a more explicit acknowledgment of boundaries. This realization begins with a self-reflection on what we deem private versus what we are willing to share, a decision that varies widely among individuals. It then extends to an awareness of others' digital thresholds, recognizing that each comment, tag, or share impacts the collective experience within these virtual spaces.

The golden rule of online interaction, treating others as one wishes to be treated, shines a light on the path of digital etiquette. This timeless principle, when applied to the digital realm, illuminates the importance of empathy and respect in every click, post, and message. It encourages a pause before sharing content related to or involving others, a consideration of how one would feel in their place. This pause, brief yet significant, becomes a bridge to understanding, fostering a culture of consent and mutual respect online. It's about seeing beyond the anonymity that screens provide, recognizing the human on the other side, and acting in ways that honor their dignity and our shared humanity.

Disagreements, as much a part of the digital landscape as they are of the physical world, demand our attention and consideration. The anonymity and distance provided by screens can sometimes embolden individuals to express themselves in ways they wouldn't in person, leading to conflicts that escalate quickly. Handling these disagreements constructively is akin to navigating a minefield with diplomacy and grace. It involves taking a breath before responding, allowing space for calm reflection rather than knee-jerk reactions. It's about choosing words with care, aiming to clarify and understand rather than to win an argument. This approach, though it may not always lead to agreement, paves the way for respectful discourse, transforming potential battlegrounds into forums for healthy exchange and growth.

Digital footprint awareness, the understanding of the long-term implications of our online actions, casts a spotlight on the permanence of digital interactions. Every post, like, and comment we make contributes to a digital legacy that outlives the momentary impulses that inspire them. This awareness prompts a thoughtful consideration of what we choose to share and how we choose to engage online. It's akin to building a monument, where each digital action is a stone in the edifice of our online presence. With this perspective, we begin to curate our digital footprint with intention, mindful of the legacy we wish to leave in the digital sands of time. This mindfulness not only safeguards our personal and professional reputation but also contributes to a digital environment that is thoughtful, respectful, and enriching for all.

In the tapestry of digital interaction, each thread of etiquette, boundary respect, constructive disagreement handling, and digital footprint awareness intertwines to create a picture of online engagement that is both respectful and enriching. As we navigate this digital landscape, let us carry with us the awareness of our shared humanity, the understanding that behind every screen lies a person deserving of respect, empathy, and kindness.

CYBERBULLYING: UNDERSTANDING AND COMBATTING

In an era where digital interactions often eclipse face-to-face conversations, the specter of cyberbullying casts a long shadow over the radiant landscape of online connectivity. This malevolent phenomenon, characterized by the use of digital platforms to harass, intimidate, or demean individuals, emerges as a pervasive challenge, leaving in its wake a trail of emotional turmoil and psychological scars. Recognizing cyberbullying involves discerning patterns of behavior that seek to belittle, threaten, or systematically dismantle an individual's sense of safety and self-worth. It manifests through venomous comments, the malicious spread of rumors, or the relentless posting of unwelcome content. Victims might find themselves ensnared in a web of digital hostility, feeling isolated and powerless, their pleas for reprieve lost in the cacophony of online noise.

To erect a bulwark against this digital onslaught requires a multipronged approach, beginning with preventative measures that empower individuals to safeguard their digital realms. Foremost among these strategies is the cultivation of a robust digital literacy, an understanding of the mechanisms and motivations behind cyberbullying. This knowledge serves as a shield, enabling individuals to navigate online spaces with an informed caution, recognizing potential threats before they burgeon into full-fledged harassment. Additionally, curating one's digital environment plays a crucial role; meticulously managing friend lists and privacy settings acts as a gatekeeping mechanism, restricting access only to those who contribute positively to one's online experience. Regular audits of online profiles eliminate personal information that could be weaponized, while fostering open dialogues about the perils of cyberbullying with peers creates a communal sense of awareness and vigilance.

When faced with the specter of cyberbullying, the response must be both immediate and strategic. The initial step involves documenting the abuse, a process of collecting evidence that not only validates the experience but also serves as a critical tool for any subsequent legal or administrative actions. Engaging with the bully seldom yields a positive outcome; instead, employing blocking features effectively excommunicates the aggressor from one's digital life, severing the channels through which they disseminate their venom. Moreover, reaching out to trusted adults or authorities offers a dual benefit—it provides emotional support while simultaneously initiating formal mechanisms of redress. These adults, be they parents, educators, or counselors, can navigate the complexities of resolving cyberbullying incidents, advocating on behalf of the victim while ensuring that appropriate consequences are levied against the perpetrator.

Supporting peers ensnared in the throes of cyberbullying extends beyond mere consolation; it is an act of solidarity that reinforces the victim's sense of belonging and worth. This support transcends platitudes, manifesting instead in tangible actions—standing alongside the victim in their quest for justice, offering a listening ear without judgment, or rallying mutual acquaintances to counteract the bully's narrative with an outpouring of positivity. Furthermore, initiating or participating in school or community programs aimed at educating about the dangers and consequences of cyberbullying imbues individuals with a sense of agency, transforming them from bystanders to advocates for a kinder, more respectful digital world.

In the crucible of online interactions, where words wield the power to uplift or devastate, the battle against cyberbullying is waged not on the individual level but through a collective commitment to empathy, respect, and action. It is a commitment to cultivating digital spaces where diversity is celebrated, dissent is expressed with civility, and all individuals can explore the vast expanses of the internet free from fear.

DIGITAL DETOX: FINDING THE RIGHT BALANCE

In the intricate dance of modern life, where screens become our stages and digital interactions our moves, the melody of connectivity plays on, unending. Yet, within this rhythm lies a hidden dissonance, a cacophony born of excess, signaling a discord between our online engagements and the essence of living. This imbalance manifests subtly at first, through the faint whispers of fatigue, a growing detachment from the tangible world, and a nagging sense of emptiness despite—or perhaps because of—constant digital companionship. These signals, often dismissed in the rush of notifications and the allure of likes, serve as harbingers of digital overload, a malaise of our times that silently erodes the fabric of our well-being.

Recognizing the need for a pause, a retreat from the relentless bombardment of information and interaction, heralds the first step toward recalibration. This pause, termed a digital detox, emerges not as an escape but as an essential recalibration, a realignment of our engagement with the digital realm. The indicators of digital overload—sleep disturbances born from late-night scrolls, a creeping inability to focus, severed from the constant pings of our devices, and a pervasive sense of disconnection amidst a networked existence—become the clarion call for action. It is in acknowledging these signs, rather than soldiering on, that we find the courage to seek silence in the cacophony, to rediscover the harmony of existence unmediated by screens.

The benefits of such a detoxification of our digital lives extend far beyond the immediate relief from the symptoms of overload. They seep into the crevices of our psyche, washing away the residues of digital fatigue, and reawakening a sense of wonder in the simple, unfiltered experiences of life. This cleansing process, though momentarily disorienting, gradually unveils a landscape of mental clarity, emotional tranquility, and a rejuvenated physical vitality, liberated from the shackles of constant connectivity. It invites introspection, a journey inward, fostering a space where creativity burgeons, undistracted by the incessant demands of digital engagement. Relationships, too, find new soil to flourish, nurtured by undivided attention and the richness of direct, unmediated interactions. The detox thus becomes a portal to a more intentional existence, where each engagement, digital or otherwise, is chosen rather than compulsive, meaningful rather than mechanical.

Embarking on this journey requires preparation, a map to navigate the uncharted terrains of time reclaimed from digital commitments. Setting realistic goals, clear in their intent and scope, marks the trailhead. These objectives, whether to reduce screen time, to engage more deeply with the physical world, or simply to rest, guide the expedition, offering checkpoints and milestones along the path. Equally crucial is the identification of alternative activities, pursuits that enrich and engage, offering sustenance for the mind, body, and soul in the absence of digital stimuli. From the simple pleasures of a book's embrace to the exhilarating call of nature's wilds, these alternatives beckon with the promise of fulfillment, drawing us into experiences that resonate with authenticity and presence.

As the detox unfolds, a transformation occurs, subtle yet profound. The initial disquiet of disconnection gives way to a serene engagement with the present, a tranquility born of simplicity. Yet, the return to digital realms is inevitable, a reintegration into the fabric of modern existence. The challenge, then, lies not in the retreat but in the balance, in weaving the threads of digital engagements into the tapestry of life without allowing them to overshadow its textures and hues. Strategies for maintaining this equilibrium abound, from designated tech-free zones, sanctuaries of presence, to scheduled intervals of connectivity, punctuating the day with periods of engagement and disengagement. Mindfulness, too, plays a pivotal role, a conscious awareness of the moment, choosing where to direct our attention with intention and purpose.

In this delicate balance, boundaries emerge as guardians of our peace, demarcating the realms of digital and physical existence. They remind us that in the vast expanse of connectivity, we possess the sovereign right to disconnect, to retreat into the sanctity of our inner worlds, unwatched, uninterrupted, and free. These boundaries, fluid yet firm, allow us to navigate the digital age with grace, embracing its gifts while remaining anchored in the essence of what it means to live fully, deeply, and truly.

In the dance of life, where the digital and the physical intertwine, finding balance becomes not just an act of self-preservation but an art form, a delicate ballet of engagement and retreat. It is in this dance that we discover the full spectrum of existence, embracing the richness of the world both within and beyond the screen.

PRIVACY AND SAFETY ONLINE: WHAT TEENS NEED TO KNOW

In the digital age, the line demarcating public from private life blurs, often leading to an inadvertent exhibition of one's personal sphere on platforms designed for an audience far beyond one's intimate circle. Navigating this terrain requires a nuanced understanding of the value of personal information, akin to recognizing the currency of one's digital data in an economy driven by information exchange. The act of sharing, seemingly innocuous, becomes a transaction with implications that stretch into the unseen future, potentially shaping one's digital legacy in unforeseen ways. Thus, a critical evaluation of what to share, with whom, and through what channels becomes imperative, a skill that demands cultivation with as much fervor as any academic pursuit.

As the digital environment evolves, so too do the methods employed by those with malicious intent, making the practice of safe browsing not just advisable but necessary. Recognizing secure websites becomes the first line of defense, a skill akin to identifying safe passages through treacherous terrain. This recognition involves discerning the subtle signs of security, from the lock symbol in the web address bar to the 'https' prefix that denotes a protected connection. Beyond this, an awareness of phishing scams, those deceitful attempts to gather personal information under the guise of legitimacy, is crucial. These threats, cloaked in the familiar garb of trusted institutions or contacts, require a discerning eye to spot and avoid, underscoring the importance of skepticism as a tool for navigating the web.

In the realm of digital friendships, the transition from online connections to real-world interactions presents its own set of challenges and considerations. The formation of friendships within the digital domain, while offering a breadth of opportunities for connection, also harbors potential pitfalls. The anonymity afforded by screens can obscure the true intentions and identities of those we engage with, making the leap from digital to physical interactions fraught with uncertainties. Guidelines for safely managing this transition involve a layered approach to vetting new acquaintances, from engaging in video calls to verify identities, to choosing public, well-populated spaces for initial meetings. These strategies, while not foolproof, provide a framework for mitigating risk, ensuring that the expansion of one's social circle into the physical realm is approached with caution and care.

The digital footprint one leaves behind, a trail of interactions, posts, and shared content, carries with it legal implications that often escape notice in the immediacy of online engagement. Awareness of the legal landscape, particularly concerning copyright infringement, illegal downloading, and the ramifications of cyberbullying, becomes a critical component of digital literacy. This awareness transcends mere adherence to laws; it embodies a respect for the creative labor of others and an understanding of the consequences that digital actions can elicit, both for the individual and for those within their digital orbit. As such, navigating the digital world with an informed perspective on these matters is not merely a protective measure but a mark of digital citizenship, reflecting a commitment to ethical engagement within online communities.

Navigating the digital terrain, with its myriad opportunities for connection, exploration, and expression, demands a multifaceted approach to privacy and safety. It requires an ongoing dialogue with oneself about the value of personal information, the vigilance to recognize and thwart threats to one's digital well-being, and the wisdom to translate online connections into real-world relationships with care. Moreover, it calls for an informed engagement with the digital world, one that recognizes the legal frameworks that govern it and respects the boundaries they set. In this, we find not limitations but the freedom to explore the digital landscape with confidence, secure in the knowledge that we are equipped to navigate its complexities safely.

As we close this chapter, the intersection of digital innovation and personal responsibility emerges as a theme that underpins our journey through the online world. The insights offered here serve as a guide, illuminating the path toward a balanced and mindful engagement with digital spaces. They underscore the importance of safeguarding one's privacy, ensuring safe browsing practices, managing digital relationships with discernment, and navigating the legal intricacies of online behavior. Together, these principles form the cornerstone of a responsible and enriching digital life, one that honors the immense potential of the internet while recognizing the responsibilities it entails. As we move forward, let these lessons inform our approach to the digital world, shaping our interactions and experiences in ways that reflect our values and aspirations.

CHAPTER 3: THE ART OF CONVERSATION

In the tapestry of human connections, the threads of conversation weave patterns of understanding, empathy, and bonds. This intricate dance of words and silences, punctuated by gestures and expressions, forms the foundation on which relationships are built and nurtured. Yet, initiating this dance often presents a daunting challenge, a moment teetering on the edge of silence and engagement. Here, in the crucible of social interaction, the alchemy of conversation starters transforms mere encounters into opportunities for connection, discovery, and mutual respect.

CONVERSATION STARTERS: BEYOND "HI"

Icebreakers that Work

Picture a room humming with the potential of new connections, a space vibrant with the anticipation of stories yet to be shared. In this setting, the right icebreaker acts as a key, unlocking doors to the castles of strangers' thoughts and experiences. One might begin with a seemingly innocuous observation, such as the unique ambiance of the venue or a piece of art adorning the wall. This approach, grounded in the immediate environment, offers a common ground from which the conversation can grow, branching out into discussions of preferences, experiences, and perspectives. Another effective icebreaker involves invoking the context of the gathering—be it a book club, a networking event, or a community workshop—to inquire about the person's interest or experience in the theme at hand. This strategy not only reveals shared interests but also demonstrates a genuine curiosity about the individual's motivations and passions.

Context Matters

Adapting conversation starters to fit the setting ensures relevance and piques interest. At a school event, for instance, initiating a conversation about a recently completed project or an upcoming holiday can immediately engage a peer, providing a familiar framework for the exchange. Conversely, at a more casual gathering, such as a party, one might opt for lighter topics, perhaps inquiring about the music playlist or a mutual acquaintance. Online, the approach shifts subtly, leveraging shared content or ongoing discussions as a springboard for conversation. The key lies in tailoring the opener to the situation, a strategy that not only enhances the relevance of the exchange but also signals attentiveness to the nuances of the setting.

Open-Ended Questions

Questions that invite more than a simple yes or no response open doors to the rich landscapes of people's thoughts and stories. Inquiring about someone's thoughts on a recent event, their experiences with a common hobby, or their aspirations for the future encourages them to share more of themselves. These questions signal an openness to dialogue, inviting a depth of exchange that transcends superficial banter. They create a space for the other person to express themselves freely, laying the groundwork for a dialogue that is both engaging and meaningful.

Listening as a Conversation Starter

Often, the most powerful conversation starter is not a question but the act of listening itself. In a world clamoring for attention, the gift of undivided attention is a rare treasure. By actively listening to someone's initial response, nodding in acknowledgment, or offering a thoughtful comment, one indicates a genuine interest in the speaker's thoughts and feelings. This attentiveness fosters a sense of being valued and understood, encouraging the speaker to delve deeper into the conversation. It's a subtle art, where silence speaks volumes, and where the act of listening becomes the bridge to deeper connection and understanding.

Visual Element: Conversation Starter Toolkit

To aid in the practical application of these concepts, envision a toolkit, neatly compartmentalized, each section brimming with phrases and questions tailored to a variety of settings and scenarios. This toolkit, perhaps presented as an infographic, offers a visual guide to initiating conversations across different contexts—school, parties, online interactions, and more. Each compartment could contain tailored openers, tips on adapting to context, and strategies for encouraging open-ended responses. Accompanying each section, brief notes on the art of listening provide reminders on the importance of this silent yet eloquent component of conversation starters. This visual element, accessible and engaging, becomes a handy reference, demystifying the process of breaking the ice and paving the way for meaningful interactions.

In the realm of human connection, the initiation of conversation stands as a threshold, a point of departure from solitude into the rich tapestry of shared experiences and mutual understanding. Here, armed with the right tools and guided by the principles of relevance, openness, and genuine curiosity, we step beyond the confines of our own worlds, venturing into the vastness of others' thoughts, dreams, and stories. It's a journey that begins with a simple "Hi" but quickly transcends it, weaving together the threads of human experience into a shared narrative of connection and discovery.

READING THE ROOM: WHEN TO SPEAK AND WHEN TO LISTEN

In the intricate ballet of social interactions, the ability to discern the subtle ebb and flow of conversation is akin to navigating a river's currents—knowing when to paddle and when to let the stream guide the vessel. This navigational skill rests on the keen observation of body language and social cues, a silent language that speaks volumes about the dynamics of a room. Like a seasoned captain sensing the change in the wind, the socially adept individual perceives shifts in group dynamics, the unspoken consensus on topics of interest, and the collective emotional climate, using these insights to steer conversations with finesse.

The foundation of this perceptual acuity is the power of observation, a vigilant awareness of the environment that transcends mere visual scrutiny. It involves tuning into the non-verbal symphony composed by those around us—the lean of interest, the fold of disengagement, the sparkle of enthusiasm in the eyes. These cues, often overlooked, are the compass by which we can gauge the receptivity of our audience, the appropriateness of our timing, and the direction in which to steer the discourse. Observing the tempo of the conversation allows for an intuitive understanding of when to interject with a contribution and when to recede, granting the floor to others. It is in this delicate balance of action and restraint that fruitful exchanges are nurtured.

Empathetic listening, then, becomes the soul of meaningful interaction. It transcends the passive reception of words, engaging instead with the emotions and intentions woven into the fabric of speech. To listen empathetically is to validate the speaker's experience, to acknowledge their perspective as both valid and valuable. This form of listening cultivates an atmosphere of trust and openness, encouraging a depth of sharing that superficial exchanges lack. It signals to the speaker that they are not merely being heard but understood, their thoughts and feelings mirrored and respected. Such a level of engagement elevates the conversation from mere exchange of information to a shared journey of discovery and connection.

The art of balancing speaking and listening within a conversation mirrors the give and take of a well-choreographed dance, where the movements of one partner complement and enhance those of the other. This equilibrium ensures that the exchange is not dominated by one voice but is instead a tapestry of diverse perspectives, each thread contributing to the richness of the whole. Strategies for maintaining this balance include mindful self-monitoring, an awareness of the proportion of time spent speaking versus listening, and the cultivation of curiosity, a genuine interest in the thoughts and experiences of others that naturally encourages more listening. Additionally, the practice of reflective listening, where one paraphrases or summarizes what the other has said before adding one's own thoughts, reinforces the value of the speaker's contribution and ensures a mutual engagement with the topic at hand.

In the realm of social interactions, the ability to read the room and modulate one's contributions accordingly is a skill of inestimable value. It opens doors to deeper understanding, fosters connections built on mutual respect, and transforms conversations into opportunities for genuine engagement and discovery. This skill, honed through observation, empathy, and a commitment to balance, enriches not only our social encounters but our broader journey through the intricate tapestry of human relationships.

SMALL TALK, BIG IMPACT: FINDING COMMON GROUND

In the mosaic of social interactions, small talk holds a unique position, often misconstrued as mere filler conversation, yet in truth, it serves as the initial brushstroke on the canvas of deeper connection. Far from being trivial, this preliminary exchange lays the groundwork for rapport, subtly weaving the threads of commonality and shared interest that can bind individuals in meaningful dialogue. It is through these seemingly inconsequential exchanges that the foundation for more profound conversation is built, an art that, once appreciated, transforms our approach to every new encounter.

The essence of small talk revolves around universal, safe topics, a repertoire that every individual can draw upon to bridge the gap between unfamiliarity and acquaintance. Weather, often joked about as the quintessential go-to for small talk, offers a neutral starting point, a shared experience that affects everyone yet holds no divisive opinions. Similarly, inquiries about food preferences or recommendations, especially in a context where eating is involved, can open avenues to discussions about culture, travel, and personal anecdotes. Local events, be it a community fair, a sports game, or a theater production, provide fertile ground for discovering mutual interests or introducing one another to new experiences. Books, movies, and music, the pillars of entertainment, serve not only as safe topics but also as windows into personal tastes, hobbies, and the emotional landscapes shaped by art. In broaching these subjects, the aim is not to fill silence but to uncover threads of similarity, to discover those points of resonance that can transform small talk from a social obligation to a bridge towards richer, more engaging conversations.

Transitioning from the surface-level waters of small talk to the deeper currents of substantial conversation is akin to navigating a ship from the safety of the harbor into the open sea. It requires both skill and timing, a keen sense of when the interaction is ready to move beyond the preliminary. One effective technique involves seizing upon a topic that emerges during small talk that hints at broader interests or deeper opinions. This could be a mention of a recent trip, a hobby, or a passing reference to work or studies. By gently probing these areas with thoughtful questions or sharing a related experience, the conversation naturally deepens, moving into territories that reveal more about values, beliefs, and personal narratives. Another method is to introduce a topic of mutual interest discovered during the initial exchange, perhaps a shared love for a particular genre of music or a common concern about an environmental issue. By linking this further discussion back to the initial small talk, a seamless transition is achieved, one that feels natural rather than forced.

The practice of small talk, like any skill, flourishes with practice. Engaging in low-pressure environments, where the stakes for social errors are minimal, provides the perfect setting to hone this art. Casual gatherings with acquaintances, volunteer events, or community classes offer opportunities not only to meet new people but to experiment with initiating and navigating small talk. In these settings, the focus should be on the process rather than the outcome, on learning to be comfortable with the ebb and flow of light conversation, and on finding joy in discovering common ground with others. Online forums and social media groups centered around hobbies or interests can also serve as platforms for practicing small talk, providing a space where shared passions naturally fuel the conversation, and the written format allows for more deliberate communication. The key is consistency and intentionality, approaching each interaction as an opportunity to refine one's ability to engage, to listen, and to connect.

Small talk, in its essence, is the art of opening doors, of inviting others into a space of mutual exploration and understanding. It is an acknowledgment of the potential in every encounter to transcend the superficial, to find common ground, and to build upon it. Through mindful engagement with safe topics, thoughtful transitioning to deeper subjects, and the deliberate practice of these skills, individuals can transform small talk from a social nicety into a powerful tool for connection. It is in these moments, often overlooked, that the seeds of lasting relationships are sown, nurtured by the willingness to engage with the world around us with openness, curiosity, and a genuine desire for connection.

THE FOLLOW-UP: KEEPING THE CONVERSATION GOING

In the realm of human interaction, the ability to maintain the flow of conversation is akin to the skill of a gardener, nurturing the delicate blossoms of dialogue with attentiveness and care. The expression of genuine interest in the words of another not only waters these blossoms but also roots them deeply in the fertile ground of mutual respect and curiosity. This authenticity in engagement signals to the speaker that their thoughts and experiences are not merely heard but valued, creating a bridge of understanding that invites further exploration.

In this intricate dance of discourse, follow-up questions serve as the steps that guide the movement, allowing the conversation to unfold with a natural grace. These inquiries, when posed with thoughtfulness, peel back the layers of a topic, revealing the rich textures beneath. They are not mere probes but markers of engagement, symbols that the listener is not only present but invested in the journey of the conversation. This form of questioning requires an active listening, a tuning in to the nuances of the speaker's narrative, searching for the threads that beg to be unraveled. Through this process, dialogue deepens, winding down paths of insight and revelation that might otherwise remain unexplored.

Sharing one's own experiences or thoughts in response to another's revelations acts as a reciprocal gesture, a give and take that is the heartbeat of conversation. This exchange, however, demands a delicate balance, a consideration of relevance and timing that ensures the shared experience illuminates rather than overshadows. When executed with finesse, this sharing fosters a sense of camaraderie, a mutual understanding that elevates the conversation from a simple exchange of ideas to a collaborative construction of meaning. It invites both parties into a space of vulnerability and trust, where personal stories and reflections are offered as gifts, enriching the fabric of the dialogue.

Yet, even in the most engaging of conversations, moments of silence inevitably arise, pauses in the melody of exchange that can either signify a breath or a break in connection. Recognizing these lulls as natural components of the conversational rhythm is crucial, allowing them to serve as spaces for reflection rather than sources of discomfort. The adept conversationalist views these pauses not as obstacles but as opportunities, moments to regroup and steer the dialogue into new territory or to allow the conversation to wind down with a sense of completion. In moments where the conversation seems to falter, a thoughtful interjection, a question, or a reflection can rekindle the flow, gently guiding the exchange back into motion. Alternatively, acknowledging the pause with understanding, perhaps with a smile or a nod, can alleviate any tension, reaffirming the connection between speakers even in silence.

In every conversation, there lies the potential for connection, for the weaving together of narratives that enrich and enlighten. The art of maintaining dialogue, of nurturing the flow of exchange from its tentative beginnings to its natural pauses, is a testament to the human capacity for curiosity, empathy, and connection. Through the expression of genuine interest, the artful use of follow-up questions, the sharing of relevant experiences, and the graceful navigation of conversational lulls, we not only keep the conversation going but also deepen our understanding of one another, forging bonds that extend beyond words.

EXITING CONVERSATIONS GRACEFULLY

The act of leaving a conversation, much like a skilled performer taking a bow after a mesmerizing performance, demands a level of finesse and awareness that leaves all parties feeling respected and valued. The subtle art of parting ways, when done with consideration, ensures the interaction's final note resonates with a sense of mutual appreciation and the potential for future dialogues. Mastering this delicate balance involves not only recognizing the opportune moment for departure but also executing the exit in a manner that honors the connection forged, however brief it may have been.

Polite Exit Strategies

Navigating the departure from a conversation gracefully requires a repertoire of strategies, each tailored to unfold with respect and politeness. A time-tested approach involves expressing gratitude for the exchange, a verbal acknowledgment that conveys appreciation for the shared time and insights. This expression, simple yet profound, serves to affirm the value of the interaction, casting the impending departure in a positive light. Another strategy lies in offering a valid reason for leaving the conversation, providing context that justifies the exit without implying a lack of interest. Whether it's another engagement that calls for your attention or a need to refresh your drink, such explanations, when offered sincerely, soften the transition and maintain the harmony of the exchange.

Timing Your Exit

The rhythm of conversation, with its crescendos and decrescendos, offers cues for identifying the optimal moment to take leave. Observing these signals requires an attunement to the flow of dialogue, seeking natural pauses or the conclusion of a topic as opportune moments to introduce the idea of parting. Initiating the exit during a lull minimizes disruption, allowing for a smoother transition that feels in harmony with the conversation's natural arc. Conversely, abrupt departures in the midst of lively exchange can jar the rhythm, leaving a discordant note in the wake of your leaving. Hence, patience and timing play critical roles, ensuring the exit aligns with the conversation's tempo, preserving its integrity.

Exiting Without Offending

The challenge inherent in concluding a conversation lies in avoiding any implication that the interaction was anything less than enjoyable or valuable. To navigate this delicate scenario involves employing language that emphasizes the positive aspects of the exchange while gently signaling the need to depart. Phrases that encapsulate the enjoyment derived from the conversation, coupled with a mention of looking forward to future interactions, frame the departure as a pause rather than an end. This approach assures the other party of their significance and the value placed on the interaction, mitigating any potential feelings of dismissal. The key lies in the sincerity of the sentiment expressed, ensuring that the departure is perceived as a necessity rather than a desire to disengage.

Following Up Post-Conversation

The conclusion of a conversation need not signify the end of the connection. The act of following up, whether through a thoughtful message, a social media connection, or a shared resource relevant to the discussion, reinforces the value placed on the interaction and the desire to maintain the connection. This gesture, reflective of attentiveness to the exchange and an interest in the individual's thoughts and experiences, lays the groundwork for deeper relationships. It transforms the transient nature of casual conversation into a stepping stone for ongoing dialogue, extending the connection beyond the confines of the initial interaction. Moreover, it serves as a tangible reminder of the encounter, a bridge to future conversations that may delve deeper into shared interests and mutual discoveries.

In the vast landscape of social interactions, the ability to depart from conversations with grace and consideration stands as a testament to one's respect for the nuances of human connection. It underscores the recognition that every exchange, no matter how brief, holds the potential for impact, shaping perceptions and fostering relationships. Mastering the art of graceful exits, therefore, is not merely a social nicety but a profound acknowledgment of the significance of every interaction and the potential it holds for enriching the tapestry of our social lives.

As we navigate the complex terrain of human communication, the skills honed in initiating, sustaining, and concluding conversations form the bedrock of meaningful connections. These interactions, fleeting though they may be, weave the fabric of our social world, each thread imbued with the potential for understanding, empathy, and shared growth. In mastering these arts, we not only enhance our capability for effective communication but also deepen our engagement with the world around us, opening doors to new perspectives, relationships, and opportunities.

CHAPTER 4: CULTIVATING CONNECTIONS

The canvas of human connection, vast and complex, is painted with the brushes of our interactions, the colors of our emotions, and the strokes of our intentions. Within this intricate artwork, the act of making new friends emerges as both a challenge and a privilege—a process that melds curiosity with courage, empathy with expression. It is in the pursuit of friendship that we find ourselves at the crossroads of vulnerability and discovery, where the paths of two lives intersect, potentially leading to a journey shared.

MAKING NEW FRIENDS: STRATEGIES THAT WORK

The quest for companionship, akin to navigating a labyrinth, demands both a map and a keen sense of adventure. Here, we explore the corridors and chambers where potential friendships await, armed with strategies that serve as both guide and light.

Finding Potential Friends: Suggestions on Where and How to Meet

In the search for companionship, shared interests and values serve as the North Star, guiding us towards those with whom we resonate. Engaging in activities that reflect our passions—be it a book club, a sports team, or a volunteer organization—naturally positions us in the vicinity of like-minded individuals. It's in these settings, where enthusiasm flows freely, that the seeds of friendship find fertile ground. Consider, for instance, the vibrant atmosphere of a community garden, where the love for nature and commitment to sustainability draw together a diverse yet harmonious group, each member a potential friend in the making.

First Impressions Matter: Making a Positive Impact

The initial exchange, brief as it may be, lays the foundation of a potential friendship. It's the quality of openness, the willingness to share a smile, a greeting, or a genuine compliment, that can bridge the gap between strangers. Like the first ray of sun piercing through the dawn, a warm and sincere introduction illuminates the possibility of a new connection. Ensuring our approachability through body language—uncrossed arms, eye contact, and a welcoming demeanor—signals our readiness to engage, inviting others to step into the circle of our presence.

Taking the Initiative: Showing Interest in Developing the Friendship

The cultivation of friendship, much like tending to a garden, requires initiative and care. Proposing a follow-up activity, whether it's a coffee meet-up after a community event or a shared hike on a well-loved trail, demonstrates a proactive desire to deepen the budding connection. This step, simple in concept yet bold in execution, reflects a commitment to the growth of the relationship. It's in these moments, when we reach out with an invitation, that we weave the threads of acquaintance into the fabric of friendship.

Patience and Persistence: The Virtues of Friendship Building

The architecture of friendship, intricate and multifaceted, cannot be rushed. It is built brick by brick, with patience and persistence. Acknowledging that strong connections are time-crafted allows us to appreciate the gradual unfolding of camaraderie. It's the steady accumulation of shared experiences, conversations, and mutual support that solidifies the bond. In this light, persistence becomes not just a virtue but a necessity, a gentle yet determined force that nurtures the relationship through its nascent stages and beyond.

Visual Element: Friendship Building Checklist

To navigate the art of making new friends, a checklist can serve as a practical guide through the process. This tool, designed to be both informative and interactive, could include prompts such as:

- **Interest Alignment**: Identify activities or groups that align with your passions.
- **Openness Practice**: Reflect on your body language and approachability; commit to small daily acts that enhance your openness to new people.
- **Initiative Actions**: Brainstorm and commit to one proactive step this week to foster a potential friendship.
- **Patience Reflection**: Journal about a time when patience led to a meaningful outcome in your life; relate this to building new friendships.

This checklist, presented as an infographic for visual appeal and ease of use, offers a step-by-step framework for those venturing into the realm of new friendships. It acts as a beacon, guiding the way with actionable steps and reflective prompts that encourage growth and connection.

In the pursuit of friendship, we embark on a voyage of discovery, not just of others but of ourselves. It's a journey marked by the courage to reach out, the openness to share, and the resilience to build connections that withstand the test of time. With each step taken, with each hand extended in camaraderie, we weave the rich tapestry of our social world, painting the canvas of human connection with the vibrant hues of friendship.

THE ART OF EMPATHY: UNDERSTANDING OTHERS

In the intricate dance of human connections, where every step and gesture holds the potential for harmony or discord, empathy emerges as the melody that guides us towards deeper understanding and unity. This capacity to inhabit the emotional world of another, to see through their eyes and feel with their heart, is not innate but cultivated—a skill honed through intentional practice and reflection. The development of empathy, therefore, becomes a pursuit as critical as it is rewarding, unlocking doors to realms of shared experience and mutual respect that stand as the bedrock of enduring relationships.

Developing Empathy: Exercises and Practices

The cultivation of empathy begins with the deliberate practice of perspective-taking, an imaginative leap into the life and circumstances of another. Exercises designed to foster this skill often involve the exploration of fictional scenarios or real-life situations from a viewpoint other than one's own. Engaging with diverse narratives through literature and film, especially those that explore the human condition across cultures and contexts, can serve as a powerful catalyst for this expansion of perspective.

Additionally, reflective journaling, centered around the experiences of others—be it a friend's dilemma shared in confidence or a situation observed in public—encourages a deeper engagement with the emotional and cognitive processes underlying empathy. Through these practices, the muscles of empathy are stretched and strengthened, enhancing our capacity to connect with others on a level that transcends mere surface interaction.

Listening to Understand

At the heart of empathy lies the distinction between listening to reply and listening to understand. The former, a default mode for many, is marked by the anticipation of one's turn to speak, where the focus is on formulating a response rather than fully receiving the message conveyed. In contrast, listening to understand requires a suspension of this impulse, an immersion in the words and silences of the speaker that seeks comprehension before contribution. This mode of listening is active, characterized by an attentiveness that is both mental and emotional, where questions are posed for clarity, not challenge, and where the listener's presence is palpable, even in silence. This quality of engagement, where one is fully attuned to the speaker, establishes a bridge of empathy, signaling to the other that their thoughts and feelings are not only heard but valued and respected.

Empathetic Responses in Conversations

The articulation of empathy within conversation is both an art and a science, requiring a delicate balance between acknowledgment and engagement. Empathetic responses often begin with validation, a verbal affirmation of the speaker's feelings or perspective that communicates acceptance and understanding. Phrases such as "It sounds like you're feeling..." or "I can see how that situation would be..." are more than mere words; they are mirrors reflecting the emotional landscape of the speaker, affirming their experience as real and significant. Beyond validation, empathetic responses may also involve the sharing of similar feelings or experiences, not as a means of redirection but as an expression of solidarity, a way of saying, "You are not alone." In this exchange, the focus remains firmly on the speaker, with the responder's contributions serving to deepen the connection rather than shift its center.

The Role of Empathy in Relationships

Empathy, in its essence, acts as a catalyst for the deepening of relationships, transforming acquaintances into confidants, and strangers into friends. It achieves this by fostering an environment of trust and emotional safety, where vulnerability is met with compassion rather than judgment. In the presence of empathy, defenses are lowered, and genuine self-expression flourishes, paving the way for a connection that is authentic and resilient. This emotional bond, strengthened through empathetic engagement, becomes the foundation upon which lasting relationships are built. It is through empathy that we come to understand not just the joys and sorrows of others, but the common humanity that binds us, bridging divides and nurturing a sense of community and belonging that enriches all involved.

In navigating the complexities of human interaction, empathy stands as a beacon, guiding us towards deeper understanding, mutual respect, and connections that endure. Through the intentional development of empathetic skills, the practice of listening to understand, the art of crafting empathetic responses, and the recognition of empathy's pivotal role in relationships, we unlock the potential for a richer, more compassionate engagement with the world around us. In this pursuit, we not only enhance our ability to connect with others but also discover the profound joy and fulfillment that come from truly understanding and being understood.

CONFLICT RESOLUTION: NAVIGATING DISAGREEMENTS

In the intricate weave of human relationships, disagreements emerge as inevitable threads, their colors stark against the backdrop of shared experiences and bonds. These moments, fraught with potential for discord, also hold within them the seeds of growth and deeper understanding, if navigated with care and insight. The labyrinth of conflict, with its twists and turns, demands a map—a set of strategies that illuminate the path to resolution, reconciliation, and, ultimately, a stronger connection.

Identifying the Root Cause

Peeling back the layers of a disagreement to reveal its core necessitates a departure from the immediacy of the argument, a step back to gain perspective. This involves a deliberate shift from the surface-level symptoms of the conflict—the words spoken in heat, the actions taken in haste—to the underlying issues that fuel the fire. Techniques to facilitate this shift include the practice of reflective listening, where the focus is on absorbing the essence of the other's perspective, and the use of clarifying questions that seek to unearth the deeper concerns, fears, or needs at play. It is often within the unspoken, within the gaps between words, that the true heart of the matter lies. By fostering an environment where these underlying issues can surface, where the invisible becomes visible, the groundwork is laid for understanding and resolution.

Effective Communication During Conflict

The bridge across the chasm of conflict is built with the bricks of open and respectful communication, a conduit through which understanding flows. This requires a language of tact and transparency, where words are chosen not as weapons but as tools for clarity and connection. Strategies to embody this approach include the use of "I" statements, which center the speaker's feelings and perceptions without attributing blame or intent to the other. It also involves active listening, a full engagement with the other's words that signals respect and a willingness to understand. The avoidance of absolutes, such as "always" or "never," which tend to escalate tensions, is another key component. In their place, a focus on specific behaviors and their impacts fosters a dialogue that is both constructive and grounded in reality. Through these practices, communication becomes not a battleground but a meeting place, a space where differences are explored with curiosity rather than defensiveness.

Finding Common Ground

The quest for common ground amidst disagreement is akin to seeking a clearing in the midst of a dense forest—a space of respite and connection. This endeavor starts with the recognition that, despite the divergence of perspectives, shared interests and goals often lie beneath the surface. Highlighting these shared objectives provides a mutual focus, a common cause around which dialogue can revolve. The practice of compromise plays a pivotal role here, where each party's willingness to meet the other halfway acts as a testament to the value placed on the relationship over the need to prevail. Techniques to facilitate this process include brainstorming sessions where solutions are explored collaboratively, and the establishment of agreements that honor both parties' needs and boundaries. Through this collaborative effort, a path is forged, one that leads away from the thicket of conflict toward the possibility of mutual understanding and respect.

Repairing Relationships Post-Conflict

The aftermath of a disagreement, with its tender wounds and lingering shadows, calls for a period of healing and rebuilding. This phase is critical, for it is here that the relationship is either fortified or further frayed. The cornerstone of this rebuilding process is the act of apology, a gesture of humility and accountability that acknowledges the hurt caused, whether intentional or not. Genuine apologies carry within them the power to mend, to soften the edges of hurt and open the door to forgiveness. Beyond words, the commitment to change, to addressing the behaviors that led to the conflict, solidifies this process, transforming apologies from mere utterances to tangible actions. Rebuilding trust, however, is a journey that unfolds over time, through consistent and sincere efforts to honor commitments and demonstrate understanding. It is through these steps, taken with patience and perseverance, that the relationship emerges not weakened but strengthened, its foundation more resilient for having weathered the storm.

In the realm of human connections, disagreements, viewed through a lens of empathy and understanding, become not impasses but avenues for growth, opportunities to deepen the bonds that unite us. By delving into the root causes of conflict, fostering effective communication, seeking common ground, and dedicating ourselves to the repair and strengthening of relationships post-disagreement, we navigate these challenges with grace. In doing so, we affirm the enduring value of our connections, embracing the complexities of human interaction as a landscape rich with the potential for learning, healing, and enduring companionship.

KEEPING CONNECTIONS STRONG: FRIENDSHIP MAINTENANCE

In the intricate ballet of human relations, the maintenance of friendships demands a choreography that balances the delicate act of presence with the art of understanding. Amidst the ebb and flow of life's myriad demands, the sustenance of these connections necessitates deliberate actions, a testament to the value we place on these bonds. It is through the conscious effort to remain interwoven in the tapestries of each other's lives that friendships endure, blossoming into relationships that provide solace, joy, and an anchor in the tumultuous seas of existence.

Regular Check-ins: Cultivating the Garden of Friendship

At the core of sustaining any meaningful relationship lies the simple yet profound act of regular communication. This practice, akin to tending a garden, ensures that the growth remains vibrant, fostering an environment where the flora of friendship can thrive. Whether through the convenience of digital messages or the personal touch of a voice call, these check-ins act as nourishment for the relationship, signaling a mutual commitment to its health and longevity. It is in the sharing of life's minutiae, the seemingly inconsequential details of day-to-day existence, that the fabric of connection is strengthened, woven tighter with each exchange. These interactions, though brief, serve as reminders of the shared journey, a nudge to the memory that even in absence, the bond persists, resilient against the forces of distance and time.

Being Supportive: The Pillars of Reliability and Empathy

Within the realm of friendship, support acts as both pillar and beacon, a source of strength and a guide through the darkness. To stand by a friend in moments of triumph is a joy, yet it is in the shadows of hardship that the depth of the bond is truly revealed.

The act of support, therefore, extends beyond mere presence; it involves an active engagement with the friend's emotional landscape, a willingness to shoulder part of their burden and walk with them through the storm. This requires not just an empathetic ear but often a readiness to provide counsel, to offer a perspective that illuminates paths hidden by the fog of distress. It is in these moments, when the world seems to narrow to the point of suffocation, that the breath of support brings space, offering a respite that revitalizes and renews the spirit.

Shared Experiences: Weaving Memories into the Fabric of Friendship

The creation and sharing of new experiences stand as milestones in the journey of friendship, markers of time spent in the pursuit of mutual discovery. These adventures, whether they unfold on the road less traveled or within the confines of a living room, serve as threads that bind, each new memory a layer that adds depth and color to the relationship. It is through these shared moments that the essence of friendship is captured, in the laughter that echoes against the backdrop of new vistas or the comfortable silence that accompanies a shared activity. These experiences, rich with the potential for joy and growth, offer a canvas upon which the story of the friendship is painted, a narrative that is continually enriched with each adventure embarked upon together.

Dealing with Changes: Navigating the Shifting Sands of Friendship Dynamics

The only constant in the tapestry of human relations is change, a force that reshapes the landscape of friendships with the inevitability of the tides. These alterations in the dynamic, whether prompted by the physical distance of a move or the emotional distance that sometimes grows with life's diverging paths, demand a recalibration of the connection. Navigating these shifts requires a fluidity, a willingness to adapt to the new contours of the relationship while holding fast to the threads that bind. It involves an open dialogue about the changes, a conversation that acknowledges the shift without casting it as a chasm too wide to bridge. Through this communication, a new equilibrium can be found, one that respects the evolution of each individual while preserving the essence of the friendship. It is in this adaptability, this capacity to redefine the parameters of the bond, that the strength of the friendship is tested and, ultimately, affirmed.

In the intricate dance of friendship, the steps of maintenance are both deliberate and intuitive, a blend of conscious effort and natural affinity. Through regular check-ins, the pillar of support, the creation of shared experiences, and the adaptability to navigate changes, the connection is sustained and nurtured. These actions, reflective of the value placed on the bond, ensure that the friendship remains a source of joy, growth, and comfort throughout the seasons of life.

DEALING WITH TOXIC RELATIONSHIPS

In the landscape of human connections, toxic relationships loom like thorns among roses, their presence often obscured until pain reveals their true nature. These interactions, marked by a consistent pattern of negativity, manipulation, or disrespect, erode the foundation of our well-being, leaving scars that can hinder personal growth and happiness. Recognizing these harmful dynamics is the first step toward reclaiming one's peace and autonomy, a necessary act of self-preservation in the face of destructive influences.

Recognizing Toxicity

The hallmarks of a toxic relationship often manifest subtly, cloaked in the guise of concern or intimacy, making their identification a task that requires both intuition and insight. Continuous feelings of inadequacy, a pervasive sense of being drained after interactions, and a noticeable impact on one's self-esteem and happiness serve as indicators that the relationship may be more harmful than beneficial. Further signs include a lopsided dynamic where one party consistently prioritizes their needs and desires over the other's, often resorting to manipulation or guilt to maintain control. Recognizing these patterns necessitates a step back, an objective assessment of the relationship's impact on one's life, grounding this evaluation in the reality of actions and consequences rather than the mirage of words and promises.

Setting Boundaries

Establishing boundaries in the wake of recognizing toxicity is akin to erecting a fortress around one's well-being, a declaration of self-respect and a refusal to permit further harm. This process begins with clarity, defining what behaviors are unacceptable and what consequences will follow if these boundaries are disregarded. Communicating these limits to the toxic individual, though daunting, is essential, delivering this message with assertiveness and conviction. It's crucial, too, to enforce these boundaries consistently, a practice that may require limiting or ceasing contact altogether. This act of self-preservation, though often fraught with difficulty, underscores a commitment to one's mental and emotional health, serving as a shield against the corrosive impact of toxic dynamics.

Seeking Support

The journey away from toxic relationships is one that need not be walked alone. Seeking support from trusted individuals—friends, family members, or professionals—provides not just solace but a perspective untainted by the fog of emotional involvement. These allies offer validation, understanding, and guidance, their insights a beacon in the tumultuous process of disentanglement. Moreover, support groups and counseling services offer a structured environment for healing, providing tools and strategies to cope with the aftermath of toxic interactions. This network of support acts as a scaffold, bolstering one's resolve and facilitating the journey toward recovery and self-discovery.

Moving On

The act of distancing oneself from a toxic relationship marks the beginning of a profound period of self-reflection and regeneration. This phase, while often marked by a spectrum of emotions—from grief for what was lost to relief at the newfound peace—offers fertile ground for personal growth. It's an opportunity to rediscover one's values, interests, and aspirations, free from the shadow of another's influence. Engaging in activities that nurture the soul, seeking out positive and uplifting connections, and practicing self-compassion become pillars upon which a new sense of self is built. This process of moving on, though punctuated by challenges, paves the way for a life marked by healthier relationships, a stronger sense of self, and a deeper capacity for joy.

In navigating the realm of human connections, the awareness and resolution of toxic relationships emerge as critical components of our journey toward well-being and fulfillment. Recognizing the signs of harmful dynamics, asserting boundaries, seeking support, and embracing the process of moving on are steps that, though difficult, lead us toward reclaiming our peace and autonomy. This path, while arduous, illuminates the strength within us, the resilience to overcome adversity, and the capacity to forge connections that enrich rather than diminish our lives. As we close this exploration of navigating relationships, let us carry forward the lessons learned, not as burdens but as beacons—guiding us toward a future of more meaningful and positive interactions, and paving the way for a deeper understanding of the complexities that define our shared humanity.

CHAPTER 5: BREATHING LIFE INTO SOCIAL CONFIDENCE

Amidst the tumultuous waves of social interactions, where the currents of conversation and the tides of public opinion can sway even the sturdiest of ships, there lies a simple yet powerful anchor: breathing. It is an action so fundamental to our existence that its potential as a tool for tranquility and focus in the throes of social anxiety often goes unnoticed. Yet, when wielded with intention, the act of breathing transforms, becoming a bridge over turbulent waters, guiding us to a state of calm from which confidence can emerge.

BREATHING TECHNIQUES FOR ANXIETY CONTROL

The Science of Breathing

The physiological underpinnings of deep breathing exercises unveil a fascinating interplay between the body and mind, where each breath holds the power to counteract the body's anxiety response. At the heart of this interaction lies the autonomic nervous system, a dual-component system where the sympathetic division primes the body for action ("fight or flight"), and the parasympathetic division cues relaxation ("rest and digest"). Deep breathing exercises stimulate the latter, lowering heart rate, reducing blood pressure, and signaling the brain to dial down stress levels. This process, known as the relaxation response, not only combats the immediate sensations of anxiety but also cultivates a general state of calmness, making it easier to navigate social waters with grace.

Practical Exercises

For those standing on the shores of social engagements, feeling the waves of anxiety lapping at their feet, a series of deep breathing techniques can serve as a lifeline. One such technique is diaphragmatic breathing, a method that emphasizes full engagement of the diaphragm, resulting in deeper, more efficient breaths. To practice, one simply places a hand on the belly and another on the chest, breathing in deeply through the nose, ensuring the diaphragm—not the chest—rises, and then exhaling slowly through the mouth. Another technique, the 4-7-8 method, involves inhaling for four counts, holding the breath for seven counts, and exhaling for eight counts, a rhythm that promotes relaxation and focus. These exercises, when practiced regularly, become tools in the social toolkit, ready to be drawn upon when the seas of interaction grow choppy.

Incorporating Breathing into Daily Routine

Integrating these breathing exercises into daily life ensures they become second nature, a reflex action drawn upon when navigating social settings. This integration can be as simple as setting aside a few minutes each morning to practice, creating a calm foundation for the day ahead. Alternatively, incorporating breathing exercises into regular activities—such as during a commute or while waiting in line—embeds this practice into the fabric of daily life, making it more accessible when anxiety begins to rise. Over time, these moments of intentional breathing build a reservoir of calm, a resource to draw upon in times of need.

Breathing Before Social Events

The moments before stepping into a social engagement, when the heart races and the mind whirls with possibilities, present a prime opportunity for the application of deep breathing exercises. Taking a few minutes to engage in diaphragmatic breathing or the 4-7-8 method can serve as a reset, a way to center oneself before crossing the threshold into interaction. This pre-event practice not only reduces anxiety but also sharpens focus, allowing one to enter the social arena with a sense of calm and presence. It is a simple act, yet its impact on social confidence is profound, transforming the approach to interactions from one of trepidation to one of anticipation.

Visual Element: Step-by-Step Breathing Exercise Guide

A visually engaging infographic that outlines the steps for diaphragmatic and 4-7-8 breathing exercises provides a quick and accessible reference for those seeking to incorporate these techniques into their routine. This guide, complete with illustrations that demonstrate proper posture and hand placement, serves as a visual anchor for the practice, simplifying the process and encouraging regular engagement. Accompanied by brief tips on integrating these exercises into daily activities and using them as preparation for social events, the infographic becomes not just an instructional tool but a beacon of encouragement for those navigating the social seas.

In the vast ocean of social interactions, where undercurrents of anxiety threaten to unsettle, the practice of intentional breathing emerges as a guiding star. It is a reminder that within each of us lies the power to calm the waters, to steer our ships with confidence, and to navigate the complexities of connection with poise and presence. Through the science-backed techniques of deep breathing, the integration of these practices into our daily lives, and the strategic use of breathing as a preparatory tool for social engagements, we equip ourselves with a potent strategy for overcoming social anxiety, fostering a sense of calm from which genuine confidence can flourish.

VISUALIZATION FOR SOCIAL CONFIDENCE

In the tapestry of mental strategies designed to enhance social prowess, visualization stands out as a technique of unparalleled potency. This method, rooted in the practice of crafting vivid mental images of successful outcomes, serves as a scaffold upon which the edifice of social confidence is constructed. The power of visualization lies in its ability to forge a mental blueprint of reality, a rehearsal space where the mind can traverse the landscape of social interactions with ease and assurance. Within this mental arena, the barriers erected by anxiety and self-doubt are dismantled, replaced by a narrative of competence and composure.

Creating a Positive Vision

The initial step in harnessing the transformative potential of visualization involves the cultivation of a positive vision, a detailed mental construct of oneself navigating social situations with a blend of ease and enthusiasm. This envisioning process begins with the selection of a specific scenario—a conversation at a gathering, a presentation before peers, or any other context that typically triggers unease. With the scenario in focus, the mind's eye pictures a version of oneself imbued with confidence, engaging with others in a manner marked by fluency and warmth. Every nuance, from the tone of voice to the choice of words, from posture to the exchange of smiles, is painted with precision in the mind's canvas. This vivid depiction does more than merely simulate an interaction; it rewrites the script of social engagement, embedding expectations of success in the psyche.

Combining Visualization with Positive Affirmations

To amplify the efficacy of visualization, it is intertwined with the practice of positive affirmations, statements that affirm one's abilities and worth. This synergy between visualization and affirmations acts as a double helix, where each reinforces the other, solidifying the belief in one's social competence. As the mental image of successful interaction unfolds, affirmations such as "I communicate with clarity and confidence" or "I am at ease in social settings" serve as the soundtrack to the visualization. This confluence of imagery and affirmation imbues the envisioned scenario with a sense of inevitability, transforming the imagined success from a possibility to a foregone conclusion.

Regular Practice for Effectiveness

The transformation of visualization from a mere exercise to a potent tool in the arsenal against shyness hinges on regular practice. Consistency in engaging with this mental rehearsal ensures that the neural pathways associated with positive social interaction are strengthened, making the transition from imagined confidence to real-world composure more seamless. Setting aside time each day for visualization, particularly before social events, embeds this practice into the rhythm of daily life, ensuring that the mind is primed for success when actual social situations arise. Over time, the regular invocation of positive social outcomes through visualization cultivates an internal environment where confidence flourishes, gradually eroding the foundations of social anxiety.

Visualization as a Rehearsal Tool

Beyond its role as a beacon of confidence, visualization serves as a rehearsal tool, a mechanism through which one can mentally navigate the dynamics of upcoming social events. This preparatory function of visualization involves not just the crafting of a positive outcome but also the anticipation of potential challenges and the strategizing of responses. In the safety of the mind's rehearsal space, one can explore various conversational paths, experiment with different approaches to interaction, and even practice recovery from faux pas. This rehearsal goes beyond the mere scripting of exchanges to include the emotional preparation for the event, ensuring that when the moment arrives, one is not only equipped with a repertoire of responses but also fortified against the tide of nerves that often accompanies social engagements.

In this landscape of mental preparation, visualization emerges as a lighthouse, guiding the way toward a reality where social interactions are navigated not with trepidation but with a sense of anticipation and confidence. Through the meticulous construction of positive visions, the reinforcement of these visions with affirmations, the commitment to regular practice, and the strategic use of visualization as a rehearsal tool, the journey toward social confidence becomes not just imaginable but achievable. With each mental rehearsal, the chains of shyness are loosened, replaced by the wings of assurance that enable one to soar in the realm of social engagement.

MANAGING REJECTION: IT'S NOT ABOUT YOU

The tapestry of human interaction, rich with the threads of connection and the hues of shared experiences, inevitably includes the stark lines of rejection. This universal encounter, woven into the very fabric of social engagement, stands not as a testament to personal inadequacy but as a rite of passage through which growth and understanding can flourish. To disentangle oneself from the immediate sting of rejection requires a shift in perspective, a reframing that positions this experience not as a marker of failure but as a milestone in the broader narrative of personal development.

Rejection, in its myriad forms, from the unreturned message to the declined invitation, echoes with the message that not all attempts at connection will find their desired harbor. Yet, this fact, rather than serving as a deterrent, illuminates the nature of human relationships—complex, subjective, and varied. Recognizing rejection as a shared human experience liberates one from the shackles of personal blame, allowing the realization that this phenomenon is less a reflection of individual worth and more an artifact of circumstance, preference, and timing. In this light, rejection assumes a less ominous form, appearing instead as a signpost along the path of social navigation, indicating not a dead-end but a fork, guiding one towards alternative routes ripe with potential.

The process of reframing rejection begins with the acceptance of its inevitability, a concession that, in the pursuit of meaningful connections, encounters of non-reciprocity are not only possible but probable. This acknowledgment sets the stage for a shift in perception, where each instance of rejection is viewed through the lens of opportunity—a chance to glean insights, to refine approaches, and to strengthen resilience. Techniques such as cognitive restructuring, where negative thoughts spurred by rejection are systematically challenged and replaced with more balanced and constructive reflections, facilitate this shift. By dissecting the experience, identifying the external factors at play, and recognizing the limits of personal control, the narrative surrounding rejection transforms. It becomes a story not of personal inadequacy but of adaptability and perseverance.

Building resilience to rejection is akin to fortifying a vessel against the storms of the sea. It demands both preparation and practice, a combination of preemptive measures and reactive strategies that together weave a bulwark against the tempest of disapproval. Preparation involves the cultivation of self-esteem independent of external validation, an anchoring in one's worth and capabilities that remains steadfast in the face of external judgments. Practice, on the other hand, involves the active seeking of situations where rejection is a possibility, a deliberate stepping into the arena of uncertainty. With each encounter, the edges of fear dull, the anticipation of rejection loses its grip, and the capacity to navigate these experiences with composure and clarity strengthens. Support systems play a crucial role in this process, offering not only solace in moments of disappointment but also perspectives that challenge personal biases and encourage persistence.

The narratives of those who have navigated the churning waters of rejection and emerged not only unscathed but enriched are beacons for those still finding their way. These stories, diverse in their details but unified in their themes of resilience and growth, offer invaluable lessons. They underscore the reality that rejection, while an inevitable companion along the journey of social engagement, is neither an end nor a definition but a waypoint. Individuals who have used rejection as a catalyst for self-reflection and development exemplify the potential for transformation that lies within these experiences. Whether it's the author whose manuscript faced countless rejections before finding a publisher or the entrepreneur who was turned away by investors only to refine their pitch and ultimately succeed, these narratives share a common thread—the recognition of rejection as not a barrier but a stepping stone.

In these stories, and indeed, in the very process of managing rejection, lies a profound truth: that the value of one's endeavors, the worth of one's self, is not diminished by the refusal of others to engage. Instead, each encounter with rejection serves as an opportunity to reassert one's commitment to personal growth, to refine the understanding of social dynamics, and to continue the pursuit of connections with resilience and insight. Rejection, then, becomes not a shadow cast over the landscape of social interaction but a sculptor, shaping the contours of character and resilience with each stroke.

STEPPING OUT OF YOUR COMFORT ZONE SAFELY

The landscape of personal growth, rich with its peaks and valleys, demands not only the courage to confront unknown territories but also the wisdom to navigate them with care. At the heart of this exploration lies the concept of stepping beyond the confines of comfort, a territory marked by the familiar and the predictable. This act, often perceived as daunting, holds within it the seeds of transformation, enabling individuals to transcend limitations and embrace the full spectrum of their potential. It is within this delicate balance of challenge and security that true growth flourishes, transforming the daunting into the achievable.

In the pursuit of self-expansion, the philosophy of incremental advancement serves as a guiding principle, advocating for a progression that is both deliberate and measured. This approach, rooted in the understanding that small, incremental steps accumulate into significant change, encourages individuals to extend just beyond their comfort zones without precipitating into the realm of overwhelming anxiety. For example, someone who finds group settings intimidating might begin by engaging in one-on-one interactions, gradually increasing the number of people as their confidence builds. Similarly, a person hesitant to voice their opinion might start by sharing their thoughts in smaller, more intimate gatherings before stepping into larger forums. This gradual escalation ensures that each step, though slightly discomforting, remains within the bounds of manageability, fostering a sense of achievement that propels further exploration.

Creating a safety net, both emotional and social, provides a critical foundation for venturing beyond familiar grounds. This safety net, woven from the threads of supportive relationships, self-awareness, and preparedness, serves as a fallback, a source of reassurance in moments of uncertainty. Cultivating relationships with individuals who offer encouragement and understanding creates an environment where risks feel less daunting, knowing there is a community to lean on in moments of doubt. Simultaneously, fostering self-awareness through reflection and mindfulness practices equips individuals with a deeper understanding of their responses to discomfort, enabling more informed decisions about when and how to push boundaries. Preparedness, achieved through research and planning, further reduces the perceived risk of new ventures, ensuring that steps outside the comfort zone are taken with eyes wide open.

The act of recognizing and celebrating each venture beyond the edge of comfort underscores the significance of these moments, transforming them from mere experiences into milestones of growth. This recognition, whether manifested through self-reflection, journaling, or sharing achievements with others, serves as a powerful reinforcement, validating the effort and courage involved in stepping into the unknown. It acknowledges not just the action taken but the bravery, resilience, and persistence that underlie it. For instance, someone who challenges their fear of public speaking by presenting to a small group should take a moment to acknowledge this act of bravery, reflecting on the courage it took to stand before others and the growth that ensued from the experience. Celebrating these victories, regardless of their size, cultivates a mindset of appreciation for the journey of self-expansion, recognizing each step as a testament to the individual's capacity for growth and resilience.

In navigating the terrain of personal development, the journey beyond the comfort zone emerges as a path marked by both challenge and discovery. It is a journey that requires not just the willingness to encounter discomfort but also the foresight to approach these encounters with strategy and support. Through the adoption of a small steps approach, the cultivation of a safety net, and the practice of celebrating each victory, individuals equip themselves with the tools necessary for safe exploration. This methodology ensures that the venture beyond the familiar is not a leap into the abyss but a measured stride into a landscape brimming with potential, where the boundaries of self are expanded and the horizon of possibility is broadened.

FROM SHY TO SOCIABLE: A GRADUAL TRANSFORMATION

In the nuanced spectrum of social dynamics, the progression from shyness to sociability unfolds not as an abrupt leap, but as a deliberate evolution, marked by intention and nurtured by a series of practical steps. This metamorphosis demands not only a commitment to change but also a mindful approach to the cultivation of social skills, where small victories accumulate to forge a path to confidence.

Setting Realistic Goals

The inception of this transformation is rooted in the establishment of goals that are both tangible and achievable. These objectives act as beacons, illuminating the path forward, guiding actions and measuring progress. For an individual navigating the complexities of shyness, such goals might range from initiating a conversation with a stranger to joining a group activity. The key lies in framing these objectives in a way that stretches the comfort zone without straining it, ensuring each goal is imbued with a sense of attainability. It is through this careful calibration of challenges that momentum is maintained, each step forward building upon the last, cumulatively expanding the boundaries of one's social capabilities.

Tracking Progress

The journey towards sociability is enriched by the act of documenting progress, a practice that serves both as a mirror reflecting growth and a map charting the way forward. Maintaining a journal or log of social interactions offers a tangible record of experiences, challenges faced, and successes achieved. This record, detailed in its accounting, allows for the visualization of improvement over time, turning abstract perceptions of change into concrete evidence of development. Moreover, this process of documentation fosters a reflective space, where insights can be gleaned, strategies refined, and motivation renewed. In the act of recording, one finds not only a tool for measurement but also a source of encouragement, a reminder of how far one has come and a spur to continue.

Finding Supportive Communities

Central to the narrative of becoming more sociable is the discovery and engagement with groups that offer a nurturing environment for growth. Such communities, characterized by their inclusivity and understanding, provide a safe harbor for those wrestling with shyness, a space where the fear of judgment is allayed by the warmth of acceptance. Identifying these groups requires a blend of research and exploration, from online forums dedicated to shared interests to local clubs that encourage participation at all levels of experience. The act of joining these communities, while daunting, opens the door to a world of interaction, where the commonality of interests fosters a sense of belonging. It is within these supportive networks that the seeds of confidence are sown, watered by the encouragement of peers and the shared journey towards personal growth.

Patience and Self-Compassion

At the core of this transformation lies the dual principles of patience and self-compassion, virtues that underpin the entire process. The evolution from shyness to sociability is inherently gradual, marked by fluctuations and setbacks that test resolve. It is here that patience asserts its value, reminding one that progress is often imperceptible in the moment, visible only in retrospect. Coupled with this patience is the need for self-compassion, a gentle acknowledgment of one's efforts and struggles. This self-directed kindness acts as a balm, soothing the sting of setbacks and bolstering the spirit in the face of challenges. It is through the application of patience and self-compassion that resilience is built, ensuring that the journey towards sociability is not derailed by the inevitable obstacles that arise.

In navigating the transition from shyness to sociability, the strategies outlined here serve as a compass, directing actions and illuminating the path to confidence. From the setting of realistic goals to the meticulous tracking of progress, from the nurturing embrace of supportive communities to the foundational virtues of patience and self-compassion, each element plays a critical role in the evolution of one's social landscape. Together, they construct a framework within which individuals can flourish, transforming the daunting into the attainable, and the solitary into the social.

As we draw this chapter to its close, it becomes clear that the journey from introversion to a more outgoing demeanor is not a solitary venture but a shared venture, illuminated by the collective wisdom of those who walk the path. The strategies delineated, grounded in practicality and infused with empathy, offer a roadmap for those seeking to enrich their social tapestry. In this progression, we are reminded of the universal nature of growth, a process that unites us in our pursuit of connection and understanding. With this foundation in place, we turn our gaze to the horizon, ready to explore the next chapter in our ongoing exploration of human interaction, armed with the tools and insights to navigate the complexities of our social world.

LET OTHERS KNOW THEY ARE GOOD ENOUGH, JUST AS THEY ARE

Great communication begins with connection.

— OPRAH WINFREY

When you enter into your teen years, there are so many things you are expected to "get right," and sometimes they can seem contradictory. You want to make friends and fit in, but also be true to yourself and defend your boundaries. You want to be authentic, while also mastering the practical social skills that enable you to connect with others and build lasting friendships. It's all a little complicated, and when you have to work it all out yourself, it can feel like you're trying to solve a puzzle that keeps getting larger and more complex.

I hope that by this stage in your reading, you've seen that when you put self-acceptance first, the pieces fall into place. Skills such as creating a good balance between your digital and real friendships, striking up a conversation with someone new, and making new friends are all a lot easier when you see relationships as a means to share the spectacular *you* with others. The aim isn't to get it right the first time around, but rather, to experiment with new strategies, learn what works and what doesn't, and hone your social skills at a steady yet unrushed pace.

If you find that this book has helped you bring your best self to your relationships, then I hope you can share your thoughts so that the teens who feel lost or lonely can unlock the key to connection.

Simply by leaving a short review on Amazon, you'll point other teens in the direction they need to make confident strides in their social lives, both in-person and in the digital sphere.

So many teens believe that they are the only ones who are struggling to build meaningful bonds. You can show them that they're not alone, simply by sharing your opinion and a little bit about what being a teen is like for you.

Thank you for your support. Together, we can help others feel stronger, more confident, and more capable of building healthy, lasting bonds with others.

Scan the QR code below:

CHAPTER 6: NAVIGATING PEER INFLUENCE

A leaf, when caught in a stream, finds itself at the mercy of the current's whims. Similarly, teens often find themselves adrift in the flowing rivers of social dynamics, where the undercurrents of peer pressure can guide them into uncharted waters. This chapter explores the psychological bedrock of peer pressure, distinguishing between its overt and covert manifestations, and the thin line separating it from positive influences. With personal values as a compass, navigating these waters becomes a less daunting task.

UNDERSTANDING PEER PRESSURE: THE WHY BEHIND IT

Psychology of Peer Pressure

At its core, peer pressure stems from a primal yearning for acceptance paired with a dread of exclusion. This potent combination can sway decision-making, pushing individuals toward choices that mirror their peers'. A study published in

"Developmental Psychology" illustrates how teens' brains are uniquely wired to value peer opinions highly, sometimes even above their own assessments or the advice of adults. This inclination towards conformity is not merely a social strategy but a neurological response to communal living, deeply ingrained in our evolutionary path.

Recognizing Different Forms of Peer Pressure

Peer pressure wears many masks, from the explicit taunts used to goad someone into trying something harmful to the subtler, perhaps more insidious, forms where mere presence or the success of peers compels one to conform. Consider the scenario of a teen faced with a group of friends who frequently skip class. The decision to join them might not stem from a direct challenge or invitation but rather from an internal calculation of the social costs of non-conformity versus the perceived benefits of belonging.

Peer Pressure vs. Positive Influence

The line between peer pressure and positive influence blurs easily. While both can sway behavior, their roots and outcomes often diverge significantly. Positive influence fosters growth, encouraging aspirations towards betterment. Peer pressure, in contrast, often nudges towards risky behaviors or choices that stray from one's values. Distinguishing between the two hinges on discernment—a critical evaluation of the motivations behind peer actions and their alignment with personal goals and values.

Personal Values as a Compass

Strong personal values offer a steadying force amid the tumultuous seas of peer influence. Just as a compass provides direction to a sailor navigating through fog, a well-defined set of values guides teens in making decisions that reflect their true selves, irrespective of external pressures. Engaging in activities that reinforce these values, such as volunteering for causes they believe in or pursuing interests that resonate with their core beliefs, strengthens their resolve against conforming to the crowd.

Interactive Element: Values Clarification Exercise

To solidify personal values, engage in a values clarification exercise. This activity involves listing values believed to be important, like honesty, courage, or compassion. Next, reflect on recent decisions or actions to assess their alignment with these values. This exercise, done regularly, sharpens the ability to make choices that resonate with one's authentic self, acting as a bulwark against undue peer influence.

By understanding the underlying psychology of peer pressure, recognizing its varied forms, and distinguishing it from positive influences, teens can navigate their social worlds with greater assurance. Armed with a clear set of personal values, the journey through the intricate landscape of peer relations becomes less about conformity and more about authenticity. This chapter lays the groundwork for exploring strategies to assert one's choices confidently, counteract bullying, build supportive networks, and empower oneself in the face of adversity, topics that we will explore in the following sections.

SAYING "NO" WITH CONFIDENCE

In the vast landscape of teenage social dynamics, the act of saying "no" stands as a testament to one's autonomy, a declaration of self-respect amidst the swirling tides of peer influence. This assertion, simple in its structure yet profound in its implications, requires a foundation rooted in assertiveness, a skill not inherent but cultivated through intentional practice and self-reflection. The journey towards embodying this assertiveness embarks from understanding its essence—not as aggression but as the respectful expression of one's needs, desires, and limits.

Assertiveness Training

At the heart of developing this crucial skill lies the embrace of assertiveness training, a structured approach designed to equip individuals with the tools necessary for clear, confident communication. This training introduces techniques such as the use of "I" statements, a linguistic shift that places the speaker's feelings and thoughts at the forefront, minimizing defensiveness in the listener. For instance, instead of succumbing to peer pressure with a begrudging yes, one might say, "I feel uncomfortable with this, so I'm going to pass." Such methods not only empower the speaker but also foster an environment of mutual respect, where the autonomy of each individual is acknowledged and honored.

Role-playing Scenarios

To refine this newfound assertiveness, role-playing emerges as a powerful tool, simulating real-life social interactions within a controlled, supportive setting. These scenarios, ranging from declining an invitation to an unwelcome event to standing firm against a group's consensus, provide a rehearsal space free from the stakes of actual social consequences. Participants, guided by a facilitator or a trusted peer, navigate these interactions, experimenting with tone, wording, and body language. Feedback in these sessions acts as a mirror, reflecting the effectiveness of communication strategies and highlighting areas for growth. Through repeated practice, the discomfort once associated with saying "no" diminishes, replaced by a sense of competence and self-assurance.

The Power of a Positive No

Within the nuanced art of declination lies the concept of the positive no, a strategy that balances refusal with the preservation of relationships. This approach, characterized by its emphasis on positive communication, seeks to decline offers without closing doors, maintaining the goodwill between peers. It involves three key components: an affirmation of the relationship, a clear refusal of the request, and, where possible, an alternative suggestion. For example, responding to a peer's proposal with, "I really value our time together, but I'm not up for that. Maybe we could try [alternative activity] instead?" achieves this delicate balance. By anchoring the refusal in the context of ongoing camaraderie, the positive no mitigates potential fallout, ensuring the bridge between individuals remains intact.

Finding Alternative Suggestions

Proposing alternatives plays a pivotal role in the landscape of saying "no," transforming the moment of refusal into an opportunity for collaborative problem-solving. This tactic not only softens the impact of rejection but also opens avenues for future interactions that align more closely with one's comfort and values. The creativity involved in crafting these alternatives requires a keen understanding of the dynamics at play, identifying activities or solutions that meet the underlying needs or desires of both parties. Whether suggesting a quiet night in lieu of a bustling party or recommending a community service project as an alternative to risky behavior, the goal remains the same: to find common ground that respects the limits of all involved.

In the intricate dance of social interactions, where the pressure to conform often clashes with the quest for authenticity, the ability to say "no" with confidence serves as a critical skill, a shield against the erosion of self-respect. Through the avenues of assertiveness training, role-playing, the strategic issuance of positive no's, and the thoughtful proposition of alternatives, this skill is honed, sculpting individuals who navigate their social worlds not on the terms of others, but on their own. In this realm, the act of saying "no" transforms from a moment of potential conflict to one of empowerment, a step towards the cultivation of relationships and self-identities grounded in mutual respect and genuine connection.

STRATEGIES TO COUNTERACT BULLYING

In the dimly lit corridors of adolescence, where shadows of doubt and insecurity loom large, the specter of bullying often emerges as a formidable antagonist. This persistent plague, manifesting in both physical spaces and the digital realm, inflicts wounds not readily visible, etching scars deep within the psyche. To delineate the contours of bullying is to recognize its multifaceted nature; it is a behavior that seeks to intimidate, belittle, or coerce, thriving on an imbalance of power. From the overt aggression of physical confrontations to the subtle venom of verbal insults and the pervasive reach of cyberbullying, its forms are legion, each variant insidious in its capacity to erode self-worth and peace of mind.

The initial response to bullying, critical in its immediacy, demands a blend of tact and resilience. In the immediate aftermath of a bullying incident, the impetus lies in maintaining one's composure, a task Herculean in its emotional demand yet vital for the preservation of dignity. A firm, unequivocal stance, devoid of aggression yet assertive in its delivery, serves as the first line of defense, signaling to the aggressor the ineffectiveness of their tactics. This response, when coupled with strategic withdrawal from the situation, denies the bully the satisfaction of eliciting distress, effectively defusing the potency of their actions. It is within this measured retreat that safety is found, allowing for the regrouping of one's faculties and the formulation of a considered course of action.

The act of reporting and seeking assistance in the wake of bullying incidents is not an admission of defeat but a strategic maneuver, a rallying of forces against a common adversary. The discernment of when and whom to approach for help is crucial; trusted adults, be they parents, educators, or school counselors, become allies in this battle, their involvement a catalyst for intervention and change. The documentation of incidents, a meticulous record of dates, times, and the nature of the bullying, becomes invaluable in this process, lending weight to the case and facilitating the implementation of corrective measures. Schools and institutions, bound by duty and often by policy, become arenas where the issue is addressed, the bully held accountable, and the environment rendered safer for all.

Parallel to these external measures is the internal fortification of the self, a bulwark against the psychological onslaught of bullying. Self-defense, in this context, transcends the physical realm, encompassing the emotional and mental planes. To cultivate a mindset armored against the barbs of bullies is to engage in self-affirmation, a daily practice of reinforcing one's worth, strengths, and the unassailability of one's dignity. This mental self-defense, rooted in a profound belief in one's value, acts as a shield, deflecting the corrosive effects of bullying and preserving the integrity of the self. In conjunction, the acquisition of physical self-defense skills, where appropriate and under guided instruction, imbues individuals with a sense of security and agency, an assurance in their capacity to protect themselves if the need arises.

Empowerment, the ultimate antidote to the venom of bullying, emerges from the confluence of these strategies. It is born in the moment of assertive response, nurtured through the act of seeking support, and solidified in the practice of self-affirmation. This empowerment is not a destination but a continuous journey, a process of becoming that renders one not impervious to the trials of bullying but resilient in their face. The cultivation of this resilience, a dynamic interplay between external support and internal strength, transforms victims into victors, individuals not defined by their experiences of bullying but refined by their response to it.

In the labyrinthine struggle against bullying, the path forward is illuminated by knowledge, fortified by support, and paved with the stones of self-respect and empowerment. Through the application of immediate response strategies, the tactical engagement of help, and the steadfast development of self-defense and empowerment, individuals navigate the treacherous waters of bullying, emerging not tarnished but triumphant. This journey, marked by battles both won and lost, shapes the contours of character, imbuing those who walk its path with a resilience that echoes far beyond the confines of adolescence, into the broad expanse of life itself.

BUILDING A SUPPORT SYSTEM

In the intricate web of adolescence, where each thread of interaction holds potential for both connection and conflict, the construction of a robust support system emerges as a pivotal scaffold. This network, composed of peers, family members, educators, and mentors, acts not merely as a safety net but as a foundation upon which resilience, confidence, and personal growth are fostered. It's within this communal embrace that individuals find the strength to navigate the complexities of social dynamics, the reassurance to face challenges head-on, and the encouragement to pursue their authentic selves.

Identifying Allies

The initial step in weaving this network involves the discerning identification of allies, a process akin to sifting gold from gravel. These allies, whether found among classmates, within the familial circle, or among the faculty, share a common thread of understanding, empathy, and unwavering support. The act of identifying such individuals necessitates an attuned observation, a keen sense for genuine gestures of kindness, and an openness to reciprocal vulnerability. For a teenager, recognizing a peer's consistent respect for boundaries, a family member's attentive ear, or an educator's proactive inclusivity can illuminate potential allies. This discernment, though subtle in its execution, lays the cornerstone for a support system that is both resilient and responsive.

Engaging with Support Groups

Parallel to the cultivation of individual relationships is the exploration of support groups, communities bound not by circumstance but by shared experiences or challenges. These groups, whether convened in the quiet of a community center or the vastness of digital space, offer a collective solace, a chorus of understanding that resonates with one's own experiences. The act of engaging with these groups, be it through active participation or quiet observation, provides a mirror to one's struggles, reflecting not isolation but a shared journey. For victims of bullying or those wrestling with the tendrils of peer pressure, these groups serve as a beacon, illuminating paths of coping, healing, and empowerment previously shrouded in doubt. The search for such groups, guided by careful research and perhaps recommendations from trusted adults, reveals a spectrum of options, each varying in focus, format, and frequency of meetings, allowing for a tailored fit to one's needs and preferences.

The Role of Mentors

Beyond the immediate circle of peers and the communal embrace of support groups lies the unique relationship offered by mentors. These individuals, distinguished by their experience, wisdom, and a commitment to guiding others, provide a lighthouse for navigating the often tumultuous waters of adolescence. The mentor-mentee bond, characterized by its depth of understanding and mutual respect, transcends conventional support by offering personalized guidance, insights born of experience, and an unwavering belief in the mentee's potential. Securing such a mentor involves not just the courage to reach out but also the clarity to articulate one's needs, aspirations, and the type of guidance sought. This relationship, once established, becomes a pivotal axis around which personal and social development orbits, propelled by the mentor's ability to challenge, inspire, and broaden horizons.

Creating a Network of Support

The culmination of these efforts, the assembly of allies, the integration into support groups, and the engagement with mentors, results in the creation of a multifaceted support network. This network, vibrant in its diversity, functions not as a static entity but as a dynamic ecosystem, evolving in response to changing needs and circumstances. Maintaining this network demands an investment of time and energy, a commitment to nurturing each connection through open communication, mutual support, and shared experiences. It also requires a degree of organization, an awareness of the unique role each member plays within the network, and an understanding of how best to interact with and contribute to the group as a whole. Through regular check-ins, shared activities, and the exchange of insights and encouragement, the network strengthens, becoming a living testament to the power of communal support.

In the crafting of this support system, individuals arm themselves with a composite shield against the trials of adolescence. Each ally, each group, and each mentor adds a layer of resilience, understanding, and encouragement, forging a collective strength that empowers one to face challenges with confidence. This network, in its essence, embodies the communal spirit of human connection, a reminder that no one navigates the complexities of growth and self-discovery alone. Through the collaborative effort of building and sustaining these relationships, individuals not only ensure their well-being but also contribute to the well-being of others, weaving a tapestry of support that extends far beyond the immediate sphere of personal experience.

EMPOWERING YOURSELF IN THE FACE OF ADVERSITY

In the vast expanse of social interaction, where the terrain is as unpredictable as it is complex, the cultivation of inner strength stands as a beacon for those navigating the stormy waters of adolescence. This process of self-empowerment, intricate and multifaceted, demands a conscious engagement with both the internal landscape of the self and the external forces of societal influence. It is within this delicate balance that individuals find the resilience to confront challenges, transforming obstacles into stepping stones towards maturity and self-discovery.

The foundation of self-empowerment lies in the development of techniques that fortify the psyche against the erosive effects of adversity. One such method involves the practice of self-reflection, a deliberate introspection that seeks to understand personal reactions to social pressures and bullying. This reflective process, though introspective, encourages a critical examination of one's beliefs, values, and the sources of one's self-esteem. Coupled with goal setting, where objectives are delineated not by external expectations but by personal aspirations, this technique fosters a sense of agency, a conviction in one's ability to influence the course of one's life. Through these practices, individuals construct an inner citadel, resistant to the tumult of external judgment and capable of nurturing growth amidst the chaos of social dynamics.

The narrative of empowerment is further enriched by the tapestry of personal stories, tales of adversity faced and overcome. These stories, shared among peers or within the sanctuary of support groups, serve as both catharsis and instruction. They illuminate the commonality of struggle, breaking the isolation that often accompanies experiences of bullying or peer pressure. More importantly, they offer a roadmap of resilience, highlighting strategies that have proven effective in the face of specific challenges. The act of sharing these narratives fosters a connection rooted in mutual understanding and shared experience, a bond that reinforces the notion that no individual navigates the complexities of social interaction alone. This communal exchange of stories becomes a wellspring of empowerment, from which individuals can draw strength and inspiration.

Integral to the journey of self-empowerment is the practice of self-care, a concept that transcends the physical to encompass the mental and emotional realms. In the face of adversity, self-care acts as a lifeline, a means of maintaining equilibrium amidst the pressures of social interaction. Whether through mindfulness practices that ground the individual in the present, creative endeavors that offer an outlet for expression, or physical activities that bolster physical and mental health, self-care is a multifaceted approach to well-being. It encourages an alignment of mind, body, and spirit, a harmony that fortifies the individual against the dissonance of external conflict. This holistic approach to self-maintenance ensures that the individual remains centered, capable of approaching social challenges with clarity and calm.

The culmination of these practices of self-empowerment finds its expression in activism and advocacy, where personal experiences of adversity are transformed into vehicles for collective change. This transition, from individual resilience to societal impact, marks a pivot in the narrative of empowerment, where the lessons gleaned from personal struggle inform efforts to address the broader issues of bullying and peer pressure. Through activism, whether in the form of peer education, participation in campaigns for greater awareness, or the development of platforms for support and intervention, individuals channel their experiences into a force for positive change. This engagement not only amplifies the impact of personal empowerment but also contributes to the construction of a social environment where respect, understanding, and support are the norm rather than the exception.

In this intricate interplay between self-empowerment and social activism, individuals not only reclaim their autonomy in the face of adversity but also forge paths for others to follow. The techniques of self-reflection, goal setting, and self-care provide the tools for navigating the internal landscape, building resilience and self-assurance. The exchange of personal narratives offers both solace and strategy, a collective wisdom that empowers individuals to confront challenges. Finally, the leap into activism and advocacy transforms personal empowerment into a catalyst for societal change, a testament to the power of individual agency in shaping a more compassionate and understanding world.

As we conclude this exploration of self-empowerment in the face of adversity, we are reminded of the inherent strength within each individual, a resilience that thrives not in isolation but in the rich soil of community and shared experience. This journey, marked by introspection, connection, and action, underscores the transformative potential of adversity, turning challenges into opportunities for growth and positive change. With these insights as our guide, we step into the broader discussion of digital communication mastery, ready to apply the principles of empowerment to the complex dynamics of online interaction.

CHAPTER 7: DIGITAL COMMUNICATION MASTERY

In a digital era where the pulse of social interaction beats through screens, mastering the nuances of virtual communication becomes not just advantageous but necessary. This chapter unfurls the tapestry of texting etiquette, a domain where brevity meets clarity, and tone crafts perception. Amidst the rapid exchange of messages that define our conversations, the art of texting demands a finesse that balances efficiency with empathy, ensuring that the essence of our messages isn't lost in translation.

TEXTING ETIQUETTE: DOS AND DON'TS

Conciseness and Clarity

In the realm of texting, where each message flickers on the screen for mere moments before the next takes its place, the value of being clear and concise cannot be overstated. This principle, akin to the brushstrokes of a minimalist painting, where each line and color holds purpose, guides us to craft messages that convey our intentions without ambiguity. When texting about plans, for instance, stating the "who, what, where, and when" in as few words as possible not only respects the recipient's time but also reduces the room for misunderstanding. This approach mirrors the precision of a well-aimed arrow, hitting the mark of communication without the fluff that could lead it astray.

Tone Awareness

Texts, devoid of the vocal cues and facial expressions that enrich face-to-face conversations, become a canvas where words alone bear the weight of conveying tone. This digital dialogue, stripped of the nuances of spoken language, poses a challenge: how does one infuse warmth, sarcasm, or seriousness into the text without being misinterpreted? The answer lies in the mindful selection of words and punctuation, where a well-placed emoji can illuminate intent, and the choice between a period and an exclamation mark can alter perception. Consider the difference in tone between "Okay." and "Okay!"—the former might read as terse, the latter as enthusiastic. This sensitivity to textual tone ensures that the emotional timbre of our messages resonates as intended, bridging the gap between digital expression and human emotion.

Timing and Responsiveness

In the digital dance of conversation, timing plays a pivotal role, setting the rhythm that either syncs or clashes with the pace of our lives. Texting etiquette champions timely responses, a nod to the immediacy that texting implies, yet it also acknowledges the varying currents of our daily routines. The expectation for swift replies must be tempered with the understanding that life's obligations often pull us away from our screens. A message sent in the morning might only receive a reply in the evening when workday whirlwinds settle into calmer breezes. Communicating delays ("Caught up at work, will reply later!") acts as a courtesy, a bridge over the gap of waiting that fosters patience and understanding.

Respecting Privacy

At the crossroads of connectivity and privacy, texting etiquette erects a signpost of respect. In this digital age, where the forward button stands ever ready to disseminate information with the tap of a finger, restraint becomes a virtue. Before sharing a message or piece of information, pause to consider the privacy of those involved. Is consent to share granted? Does the information belong in the public domain of group chats, or is it a whisper meant for a single ear? This respect for privacy, a bulwark against the breach of trust, ensures that our digital interactions are marked by integrity, safeguarding relationships against the erosion of confidence and respect.

Visual Element: The Texting Etiquette Checklist

A checklist, visually engaging and easy to navigate, distills the essence of texting etiquette into actionable points. From the clarity of message composition to the subtleties of conveying tone, from the nuances of timing to the sanctity of privacy, this checklist serves as a quick reference for the conscientious texter. Accompanied by icons that capture the core of each guideline—a clock for timing, a lock for privacy—it transforms abstract principles into tangible practices, a compass for navigating the vast seas of digital dialogue.

In the intricate ballet of digital communication, where each message is both a step and a gesture, mastering the choreography of texting etiquette empowers us to move with grace and confidence. It is a dance that demands not just awareness of our own steps but also sensitivity to the rhythm of those with whom we share the stage. Through the diligent application of these guidelines, we weave a tapestry of interactions marked by respect, understanding, and genuine connection, a testament to the potential of digital dialogue to enrich rather than impoverish our social fabric.

SOCIAL MEDIA: CONNECTING RESPONSIBLY

In the labyrinth of pixels and posts that constitute our social media landscapes, every user stands at the helm of their digital persona, navigating through streams of content with the power to shape perceptions, influence moods, and alter relationships. This section delves into the stewardship of one's online presence, drawing boundaries between personal revelation and privacy, confronting the specter of online negativity, and acknowledging the nuanced impact of social media on mental health. Each of these facets interweaves to form a comprehensive approach to digital engagement that honors both the self and the collective digital community.

Crafting a persona that reflects one's values and aspirations while inviting positive interaction requires a delicate balance. Strategies for fostering such a presence lean heavily on the authenticity of content, the intentionality behind posts, and the cultivation of a space that encourages constructive dialogue. For instance, sharing achievements or insights that resonate with one's genuine interests not only enriches the social fabric of one's network but also invites engagement from like-minded individuals, fostering a community grounded in mutual respect and shared values. This mindful approach to social media underscores the importance of each post as a building block in the architecture of one's digital identity, a notion that encourages reflection before revelation.

However, the act of sharing, when left unchecked, tiptoes into the realm of oversharing, a territory where the personal becomes public, and privacy lines blur. Navigating this boundary demands a critical assessment of the content's impact, both on oneself and the audience. Questions such as, "Does this share enrich my digital narrative or expose too much?" or "Who benefits from this information?" become guiding lights in this process. This evaluation not only protects one's personal space but also respects the audience's time and attention, ensuring that shared content adds value rather than clutter to the communal digital space.

The digital realm, for all its potential for connection and enlightenment, harbors shadows of negativity, from the mildew of unsolicited criticism to the ice of cyberbullying. Dealing with this aspect of social media involves both armor and strategy. The armor, a fortified sense of self, repels the impact of negative comments, while the strategy, a combination of tools provided by platforms and personal policies on engagement, ensures a clean, respectful space. Filtering tools, report mechanisms, and the decisive act of blocking are utilities in this ongoing effort to maintain a healthy digital environment. Additionally, adopting a policy of non-engagement with harmful content acts as a buffer, preserving mental space and keeping the focus on positive, constructive interactions.

Beyond the immediate effects of negativity, the broader influence of social media on mental health looms large, casting shadows of doubt, comparison, and dissatisfaction. Awareness of this impact prompts a recalibration of social media habits, steering them towards healthier shores. Setting boundaries around usage, such as dedicated offline hours and curated content feeds, becomes an act of self-care, reducing the noise of constant comparison and fostering a healthier relationship with digital platforms. Furthermore, diversifying sources of validation and fulfillment beyond the digital sphere enriches one's sense of self, reducing the weight of social media's influence. Engaging in offline activities that nurture the soul, from the simplicity of a walk in nature to the joy of face-to-face interactions, reanchors one's sense of worth in the tangible and true.

Responsible connection on social media, then, emerges from the confluence of these strategies—a considered approach to sharing, a vigilant stance against negativity, and a mindful engagement with the digital world that honors the complexity of human emotion and the sanctity of personal space. In navigating these digital currents, each user becomes both a navigator and a guardian of their mental landscape, steering towards interactions that uplift and support, crafting a digital footprint that resonates with authenticity, and fostering a social media realm that reflects the best of human connection and understanding.

HANDLING ONLINE MISUNDERSTANDINGS

In the digital tapestry where threads of communication intertwine in complex patterns, misunderstandings emerge as inevitable knots, distorting the intended picture. These digital hiccups, while common, carry the potential to fray connections, necessitating a skillful approach to untangling without further damage. This section explores strategies to navigate the murky waters of online misunderstandings with tact and empathy, aiming to preserve the integrity of digital interactions and the relationships they support.

Clarifying before Reacting

In the shadow of ambiguity, where messages hang suspended between intent and interpretation, the impulse to react swiftly often overshadows the need for comprehension. This precipitous leap to conclusions, fueled by the immediacy digital communication affords, overlooks the critical step of seeking clarification. The act of pausing, a deliberate cessation of immediate response, allows for reflection on the message's ambiguity. Probing questions, poised and open-ended, invite elaboration, casting light on obscured meanings and revealing the sender's intent. This approach, akin to carefully peeling back layers, eschews assumptions, fostering a dialogue that seeks understanding above all. It is in this space of inquiry and patience that many potential conflicts find resolution, dissolving under the scrutiny of direct communication.

Apologizing Online

When misunderstandings breach the peace of digital discourse, the art of apology becomes a vital tool in the arsenal of online etiquette. This delicate craft, when executed with sincerity and humility, possesses the power to mend fissures, restoring harmony to disrupted dialogues. The key lies in the acknowledgment of one's role in the misunderstanding, a concession of fallibility that humanizes and disarms. Coupled with an expression of regret and a commitment to future clarity, this acknowledgment transcends mere words, embodying a gesture of respect towards the injured party. Crafting such an apology, devoid of excuses and rich in genuine remorse, demands an introspective honesty, a willingness to confront one's missteps and learn from them. This maturity, evident in the act of apologizing, strengthens bonds, imbuing digital interactions with a resilience against future misunderstandings.

Taking Conversations Offline

Certain digital misunderstandings, with their roots deep in the soil of miscommunication, resist resolution through text alone. In these instances, the transition from the pixelated realm to the auditory or physical, from online messages to voice calls or face-to-face discussions, becomes a bridge to clarity. This shift, a return to the nuances of spoken language, where tone, pace, and pause play pivotal roles, offers a richer medium for understanding. The choice of medium, dictated by the relationship's nature and the misunderstanding's complexity, requires a mutual agreement, a consensual step towards resolution. Engaging in this dialogue, armed with the intent to clarify and reconcile, leverages the full spectrum of communication, from verbal cues to body language, in service of understanding. It is through this synthesis of digital and direct communication that the fog of misunderstanding often lifts, revealing a path to mutual comprehension.

Preventive Measures

In the architecture of digital communication, where every message builds upon the last, preventative strategies act as the foundation, reducing the likelihood of misunderstandings from the outset. These strategies, simple yet effective, hinge on the explicit expression of tone and the judicious use of emojis as tone markers. Emojis, in their colorful simplicity, offer a shorthand for emotion, infusing texts with clear indicators of jest, affection, or concern. This visual language, when employed sparingly and appropriately, enriches texts, bridging the gap between written word and spoken emotion. Similarly, the explicit statement of tone, a brief precursor to potentially ambiguous messages ("I'm joking here:"), functions as a clarifying lens, focusing the recipient's interpretation and forestalling misreads. These measures, proactive and considerate, weave a thread of clarity through the fabric of digital discourse, minimizing the knots of misunderstanding that hinder seamless communication.

In the intricate dance of digital interaction, where steps are typed and missteps are common, the strategies outlined above offer a choreography for navigating misunderstandings. From the initial pause for clarification to the humble articulation of apologies, from the strategic shift to direct communication to the preventative clarity of expression, these approaches provide a blueprint for maintaining the integrity of digital relationships. Engaging with these strategies not only mitigates the immediate friction of misunderstandings but also reinforces the fabric of digital discourse, making it more resilient, respectful, and rich in mutual understanding.

THE ROLE OF VIDEO CALLS IN MAINTAINING RELATIONSHIPS

In an era where digital communication eclipses the warmth of face-to-face interactions, video calls emerge as the golden mean, blending the immediacy of real-time conversation with the convenience of distance. This delicate interplay between presence and absence requires a nuanced understanding of etiquette, an appreciation for the subtleties of non-verbal communication, meticulous preparation of one's digital environment, and a conscious effort to harmonize online engagements with the irreplaceable value of in-person connections.

Video Call Etiquette

Navigating the intricate dance of video call etiquette demands an adherence to a set of unspoken rules, a tacit agreement among participants to uphold the sanctity of shared digital space. Punctuality, the first pillar of this etiquette, respects the temporal boundaries of all involved, acknowledging that the digital realm does not render time any less precious. The act of joining a call at the agreed-upon moment signals respect, setting a tone of mutual consideration that defines the interaction's tempo. Within this shared space, the imperative to remain present transcends physical attendance, extending to the realm of attention. The temptation to multitask, to split one's focus between the screen and peripheral distractions, dilutes the quality of engagement, rendering interactions shallow. Maintaining eye contact, nodding in affirmation, and reacting appropriately to conversation threads weave a tapestry of attentiveness that enriches the call, fostering a sense of closeness despite geographical divides.

Visual Cues and Body Language

While words traverse the digital divide, carrying messages from sender to receiver, it is the silent language of gestures, expressions, and postures that imbue these words with depth. The ability to both convey and interpret these non-verbal cues over video calls requires a heightened sensitivity, an attunement to the flickers of emotion that dance across faces and the gestures that punctuate speech. A smile, the universal sign of warmth, bridges miles, while a furrowed brow may signal confusion, prompting clarification. This silent dialogue, a symphony of nods, tilts, and gestures, enriches communication, ensuring that the essence of messages is not lost in translation. Mastering this visual vocabulary allows participants to navigate the subtleties of digital conversations with greater acuity, ensuring that the heart of the interaction remains intact.

Technical Preparation

The foundation upon which successful video calls rest is not just the willingness of participants to engage but also the readiness of the technology that facilitates these interactions. Ensuring a smooth experience, free from the hiccups of technical malfunctions, starts with the meticulous preparation of one's digital environment. A stable internet connection, the lifeline of digital communication, minimizes disruptions, maintaining the flow of conversation. Adjusting the lighting, positioning the camera at eye level, and choosing a background free from distractions enhances visual clarity, ensuring that the focus remains on the interaction. Similarly, testing audio and video settings before the call guards against unforeseen technical issues, preserving the sanctity of the digital meeting space. This preparation, though often overlooked, is a silent contributor to the quality of video calls, a backstage hand that sets the stage for meaningful interactions.

Balancing Digital and In-Person Interactions

At the heart of our exploration lies the question of balance, of finding the equilibrium between the convenience of video calls and the irreplaceable richness of in-person interactions. This quest for harmony acknowledges that while video calls bridge distances, bringing faces and voices into our homes, they cannot replicate the warmth of a hug, the electricity of a shared glance, or the solidarity of physical presence. Striking this balance involves a conscious allocation of time and energy, a deliberate choice to engage digitally without allowing these interactions to eclipse the opportunities for face-to-face connection. It means recognizing the unique value each mode of communication brings to our relationships, using video calls to maintain connections across distances while cherishing and prioritizing the moments we can share the same physical space. This equilibrium ensures that our relationships, nourished by the immediacy of video calls, are deepened by the unspoken understandings and shared experiences that only in-person interactions can provide.

In this intricate weave of digital and physical threads, the tapestry of our relationships finds its strength. Video calls, with their blend of real-time interaction and digital convenience, offer a medium through which connections can be maintained, even flourished, across the expanses of distance. Yet, it is in the interplay between these digital engagements and the moments we share in physical proximity that the full spectrum of human connection is realized. Through the mindful practice of video call etiquette, the nuanced reading and conveying of non-verbal cues, the diligent preparation of our digital environments, and the conscious effort to balance these interactions with in-person connections, we navigate the complexities of maintaining relationships in a digital age. This dance, a blend of presence and absence, ensures that the threads of our connections, woven through both screens and shared spaces, remain vibrant and strong, testaments to the enduring power of human connection in an increasingly digital world.

ONLINE GAMING: SOCIAL SKILLS IN VIRTUAL SPACES

Within the pixelated realms of online gaming, a microcosm of broader social interactions unfolds, where players, transcending the physical confines of their existence, collaborate, compete, and commune in quests for victory and camaraderie. Here, beneath the surface of gameplay, lies a fertile ground for the cultivation of skills that, while honed in the virtual world, find profound applications in the tangible interactions of daily life.

The essence of online gaming, at its core, revolves around the synergistic dance of collaboration and teamwork. Players, cast into roles within a digital troupe, learn quickly that success is often a fruit borne of collective effort rather than individual prowess. This environment, where strategies are debated and roles assigned with precision, mirrors the dynamics of real-world team projects and endeavors. Communication, clear and purposeful, becomes the thread binding the group's efforts, a skill refined with each raid or mission. In this space, players learn not only to articulate their thoughts with clarity but also to listen, to integrate diverse perspectives into a cohesive strategy. This digital rehearsal of collaboration and communication finds its echo in the workplace, in academic group projects, and in any endeavor where success is a tapestry woven from the threads of individual contributions.

Competition, the twin flame of collaboration in the gaming world, offers its own lessons, teaching players to navigate the fine line between healthy rivalry and the corrosive descent into hostility. Within the crucible of competition, gamers confront not only the challenge of outmaneuvering opponents but also the handling of defeat with grace and victory with humility. This duality, where joy and disappointment walk hand in hand, fosters resilience, teaching players to view setbacks not as termini but as waypoints on the path to improvement. Transferring this resilience to real-world scenarios, gamers find themselves better equipped to face academic challenges, workplace setbacks, and personal trials with a steadier hand, viewing each as an opportunity for growth rather than a marker of failure.

Navigating the vast expanse of online gaming communities demands a discerning eye, one capable of distinguishing between environments that uplift and those that degrade. Choosing the right community, one that aligns with the player's values and aspirations, becomes a crucial decision, akin to selecting a circle of friends or a professional network. In these digital congregations, where behavior ranges from the noble to the nefarious, gamers learn the importance of surrounding themselves with positivity, of contributing to environments that foster respect, encouragement, and mutual growth. This selection process, while practiced in the virtual domain, mirrors the choices faced in the tangible world, where the company one keeps can significantly influence personal development and well-being.

The skills honed in the virtual arenas of online gaming, from strategic thinking to quick decision-making, hold valuable lessons for real-world application. Gamers, accustomed to analyzing complex situations, predicting opponents' moves, and making split-second decisions, find themselves at an advantage in environments that demand quick thinking and adaptability. This strategic agility, when applied to the challenges of everyday life, from navigating career decisions to resolving personal conflicts, imbues gamers with a sense of confidence in their ability to assess situations and act with both speed and precision.

In the synthesis of these experiences, online gaming emerges not as a mere pastime but as a crucible for the development of social skills that extend far beyond the digital landscape. The lessons of collaboration, competition, community navigation, and strategic thinking, each a thread in the rich tapestry of online gaming, weave patterns that find resonance in the fabric of real-world interactions. As players traverse these virtual spaces, they do so not merely as participants in a game but as architects of skills that shape their interactions within the broader expanse of their lives.

In reflecting on the journey through the digital realms of texting, social media, video calls, and online gaming, we recognize the profound influence these platforms wield on the development of social skills and the maintenance of relationships. Each domain, with its unique challenges and opportunities, offers a landscape for growth, for the refinement of communication, collaboration, and strategic thinking. As we close this chapter, we carry forward the understanding that our digital interactions, far from being mere echoes of our real-world selves, are integral threads in the fabric of our social existence, shaping and being shaped by the skills we cultivate and the choices we make. This recognition paves the way for our exploration of the next chapter, where we delve deeper into the intricacies of maintaining and nurturing relationships in an increasingly connected world.

CHAPTER 8: PREPARING FOR LIFE'S MILESTONES

Imagine standing at the edge of a forest, the ground beneath your feet a blend of paths trodden and untrodden, each leading to distinct clearings known as milestones in the expanse of life. One such clearing, often shrouded in a mix of anticipation and trepidation, is the first job interview. Here, the trees whisper of first impressions, the wind carries tales of inquiry and response, and the sun casts shadows that dance between confidence and nervousness.

THE FIRST JOB INTERVIEW: MAKING A GOOD IMPRESSION

Research and Preparation

Before stepping into the clearing, one must gather knowledge about the terrain. Understanding the company's mission, culture, and recent achievements equips you with a map to navigate the conversation. Preparing answers to common interview questions allows for a rehearsal of steps before the dance begins. Like studying the rules and strategies of chess before a tournament, this preparation sharpens your mind, making you ready for the moves and counter-moves of the interview.

Body Language and Attire

The attire you choose is your armor, and your body language, your sword. Dressing appropriately for the company's culture signifies respect and adaptability, while positive body language—maintaining eye contact, offering a firm handshake, sitting upright yet relaxed—signals confidence and engagement. A study cited in the *Journal of Applied Psychology* underscores the impact of nonverbal cues on first impressions, making the mastery of this silent language as crucial as the spoken word.

Answering Questions with Confidence

The heart of the interview lies in the exchange of questions and answers, a dance of dialogue where each step reveals more of your character and capabilities. Responding with confidence, even when discussing weaknesses, transforms perceived vulnerabilities into showcases of self-awareness and a commitment to growth. Framing weaknesses positively, as areas for development rather than insurmountable obstacles, paints a portrait of resilience. For instance, mentioning a struggle with public speaking can lead into a discussion on the steps you're taking to improve, highlighting a proactive approach to personal and professional development.

Follow-up Etiquette

As the interview concludes and you step out of the clearing, the journey continues with the art of the follow-up. Sending a thank-you email not only demonstrates courtesy but also reiterates your interest in the position, keeping the memory of your conversation alive in the interviewer's mind. This gesture, akin to watering a newly planted seed, nurtures the potential for growth—growth of opportunity, relationship, and career. Inquiring about your application status, when done politely and after a reasonable period, shows initiative and eagerness, qualities that employers value.

Interactive Element: Interview Preparation Checklist

A checklist serves as a tangible guide through the forest of preparation, ensuring no stone is left unturned. This tool, laid out in clear, actionable steps, covers everything from researching the company's background to selecting an outfit that aligns with the company culture, from practicing responses to common interview questions to drafting a thoughtful thank-you email. Each item ticked off brings you closer to making that lasting first impression, turning the daunting into the achievable.

In navigating the first job interview, a milestone that marks the transition from the realm of education to the world of work, preparation paves the path, attire and body language speak volumes, and confidence in answering questions opens doors. The follow-up, a final touch, cements the impression made, leaving a trail that may very well lead to the next clearing in the forest of life's milestones.

COLLEGE INTERVIEWS: SHOWCASING YOUR SOCIAL SAVVY

Expressing Your Unique Story

In the tapestry of a college interview, threads of diverse experiences and perspectives weave together to form a distinctive pattern that sets you apart. This narrative, your unique story, is not merely a recounting of events but a reflection of the lessons learned, challenges overcome, and the aspirations that propel you forward. Articulating this story demands introspection, a deep dive into the reservoir of your past to distill experiences that highlight your resilience, creativity, and growth. It involves framing your journey not as a series of happenings but as a deliberate path towards self-discovery and ambition. When asked to speak about yourself, view it as an invitation to unveil the chapters of your life that have shaped your character, influenced your choices, and honed your aspirations. This approach transforms the narrative from a monologue into a dialogue, inviting the interviewer to explore the depths of your experiences and the breadth of your perspectives.

Asking Insightful Questions

The art of inquiry, when wielded with precision, unveils a landscape rich in curiosity and engagement. Preparing questions to pose during the interview does more than demonstrate your interest; it reveals a mind eager to delve beyond the surface, seeking a deeper understanding of the institution's ethos, opportunities, and community. These questions, carefully crafted and thoughtfully timed, should pivot away from information readily available on the college's website, venturing instead into areas of personal significance and institutional values. Inquire about facets of student life that align with your passions, about mentorship opportunities within your field of interest, or about the college's initiatives in areas you deeply care about. This strategy not only positions you as a proactive candidate but also as a prospective member of the college community, already invested in contributing to and enriching the campus culture.

Handling Nerves

The specter of anxiety, with its cold grip and whispering doubts, often looms over the landscape of college interviews. Yet, the key to navigating this terrain lies not in the evasion of nervousness but in its acknowledgment and management. Techniques rooted in both the physical and psychological can serve as anchors, steadying you against the waves of anxiety. Deep, rhythmic breathing acts as a rudder, guiding your mind towards calm waters, while visualization techniques, where you picture a successful interview, serve to chart a course of confidence. Acknowledging nerves as a natural response to a high-stakes scenario can also diffuse their power, allowing you to reframe anxiety as a sign of your commitment and desire to excel. Practice, the act of rehearsing answers to potential questions and engaging in mock interviews, builds familiarity with the format and flow of the interview, reducing the unknowns that fuel nervousness. Through these strategies, you navigate the currents of anxiety with grace, steering towards a performance marked by poise and assurance.

Post-Interview Communication

In the aftermath of the interview, as the adrenaline fades and reflection takes its place, the importance of post-interview communication comes into focus. This phase, often overlooked, is where the seeds of a lasting impression are sown. A thank-you note, sent within 24 hours of the interview, is more than a gesture of courtesy; it is an affirmation of your interest and gratitude for the opportunity. This note should not only express thanks but also reiterate your enthusiasm for the college and the program, perhaps touching briefly on a moment or topic from the interview that particularly resonated with you. In the event of receiving an offer or, conversely, a rejection, your response should reflect not only your immediate feelings but also your professionalism and maturity. An acceptance of an offer should convey your excitement and gratitude, while a respectful acknowledgment of a rejection can leave the door open for future opportunities, demonstrating your grace in the face of disappointment. This communication, nuanced and timely, reinforces your image as a thoughtful and engaged candidate, leaving a lasting mark on the interview process.

In the realm of college interviews, where first impressions hold the power to open gateways to future academic and personal growth, the strategies outlined above serve as your compass. Articulating your unique story invites a connection, asking insightful questions displays your depth, handling nerves showcases your resilience, and post-interview communication cements your professionalism. Together, these elements weave a narrative of a candidate not only prepared for the challenges of college but also eager to contribute to and grow within its community.

DATING: RESPECTFUL AND HEALTHY APPROACHES

Communicating your intentions

In the intricate dance of dating, where emotions flutter like leaves in a gentle breeze, the act of laying bare one's intentions serves as the cornerstone of potential harmony or discord. This dialogue, often fraught with vulnerability, demands a clarity that pierces through the fog of uncertainty, ensuring that both participants stand on common ground. It is through this prism of transparency that expectations find their voice, allowing individuals to navigate the waters of connection with a map that charts a course of mutual understanding. For instance, when two souls find themselves at the crossroads of companionship, articulating whether the path sought is casual or committed can steer the journey away from the cliffs of confusion and towards the plains of peace. Such conversations, though delicate, foster an environment where honesty flourishes, laying a foundation for relationships built not on the sands of assumption, but on the bedrock of mutual clarity.

Consent and boundaries

In the realm of dating, where two worlds converge, the sanctity of consent and the respect for boundaries emerge as the twin pillars upon which a respectful relationship rests. Consent, a word that resonates with the power of autonomy, becomes the key that unlocks the door to a realm where each individual's sovereignty is revered. It is a dynamic landscape, constantly evolving with the ebb and flow of comfort and preference, demanding an ongoing dialogue that respects the ever-changing contours of consent. Similarly, boundaries, those invisible lines that encircle the treasure of one's comfort and security, demand acknowledgement and respect. Whether these boundaries delineate the physical, emotional, or digital spheres, their recognition and preservation are paramount. In acknowledging these limits, and seeking consent within their confines, individuals weave a tapestry of trust and respect, a sacred cloth that cloaks their interactions in dignity and care.

Handling rejection gracefully

Amidst the verdant fields of dating, where hopes bloom with the vibrancy of spring, the shadow of rejection looms, a reminder of the cycle of seasons that governs human connections. This specter, though often feared, carries with it lessons of growth and resilience, teaching those it touches the art of accepting refusal with the elegance of a leaf surrendering to the autumn wind. To face rejection is to face one's own vulnerability, to acknowledge it not as a verdict of worth but as a step in the dance of discovery. In this light, responding to rejection becomes an exercise in maturity, a gentle nod of acknowledgment that respects the other's choice while safeguarding one's own dignity. This response, imbued with respect and devoid of bitterness, ensures that the gardens of interaction remain untainted by the weeds of resentment, allowing for future blooms of connection to flourish unimpeded.

Building a healthy relationship

At the heart of every flourishing garden of companionship lies the fertile soil of a healthy relationship, nurtured by the rains of trust and the sunlight of open communication. Trust, that ethereal essence which binds individuals with invisible threads of confidence, grows from the seeds of consistency and reliability, watered by actions that match words and promises kept with care. It is the canopy that shelters the relationship from the storms of doubt, allowing the fruits of connection to ripen under its protection. Parallel to trust runs the river of communication, a lifeline that nourishes the roots of understanding and empathy. This stream, clear and unobstructed, carries the whispers of desires, the murmurs of concerns, and the laughter of shared joy, ensuring that no stone of misunderstanding dams its flow. In this dynamic interplay of trust and communication, a relationship finds its wings, soaring above the clouds of uncertainty into the clear skies of mutual respect and shared growth.

NAVIGATING FAMILY GATHERINGS

In the woven fabric of social interactions, family gatherings stand as intricate patterns, imbued with the threads of history, emotion, and the subtle dynamics of relationships long established. These occasions, be they celebrations of joy or congregations of solemnity, offer fertile ground for the cultivation of bonds, the exploration of shared heritage, and the occasional navigation through the brambles of familial discord.

Engaging with Relatives

The art of engaging relatives, especially those less familiar or seldom seen, mirrors the delicate process of sketching a portrait with words, where each stroke aims to reveal depth and form. Initiating conversations that transcend the mundane requires a palette rich in curiosity and attentiveness. Questions crafted from genuine interest in their lives, their passions, and their challenges open doors to chambers of shared experiences and unexplored stories. This approach not only breathes life into the dialogue but also weaves a stronger connection, turning fleeting encounters into meaningful exchanges. When faced with the reticence of a relative, patience becomes your ally. Offering snippets of your own journey serves as an invitation for them to step into the dance of dialogue, creating a reciprocity that enriches the exchange.

Dealing with Difficult Topics

Family gatherings, for all their warmth, can sometimes cast long shadows, where difficult topics lurk, awaiting their moment in the sun. The skill lies in navigating these conversations with the finesse of a leaf on the wind, aware yet untethered. When questions or topics arise that tread too closely to the borders of comfort or propriety, redirection becomes a subtle art. A gentle steer of the conversation toward common ground or lighter subjects acts as a buffer, maintaining the peace without the starkness of dismissal. For moments when avoidance is less viable, a response that acknowledges the query while firmly setting the boundary ("I appreciate your concern, but I find that topic a bit too personal. How about we talk about…?") respects both the inquirer and your own space. This tactful handling ensures the preservation of harmony, allowing the gathering to flow around potential eddies of discomfort.

Contributing to the Gathering

In the tapestry of family gatherings, every individual has the potential to contribute a thread that enriches the whole. Offering assistance with the preparations, whether through the culinary crafting of dishes or the aesthetic arrangement of spaces, not only eases the burden on hosts but also embeds you within the fabric of the event. Participation in activities, from games that spark laughter to stories that bridge generations, injects vitality into the gathering, turning passive attendance into active involvement. These contributions, though varied in form, share a common heart—they are expressions of care, tokens of belonging that strengthen the bonds of family, weaving you deeper into the collective narrative.

Setting Personal Boundaries

Amid the conviviality of family gatherings, the importance of personal boundaries emerges as a beacon, guiding the preservation of one's peace and autonomy. The delineation of these boundaries, both in the spectrum of interaction and the investment of time and energy, requires clarity both inwardly and in expression. Deciding in advance the contours of your participation allows for a balanced engagement, where involvement does not tip into the realm of exhaustion or discomfort. Communicating these limits, when necessary, with clarity and kindness ("I'm glad to be here, but I might step out for a bit if I need some quiet.") ensures respect for your needs without diminishing the spirit of togetherness. In instances where boundaries are challenged, a firm yet gentle reassertion underscores their importance, reinforcing the respect for personal space as a mutual cornerstone of family interaction.

In navigating the diverse landscape of family gatherings, where each interaction holds the weight of history and the potential for growth, the strategies outlined above serve as navigational stars.

Engaging relatives with genuine curiosity fosters deeper connections, skillfully steering conversations away from the shoals of discomfort maintains the harmony of the gathering, contributing to the collective experience enriches the communal tapestry, and respecting personal boundaries ensures the preservation of individual peace. Each of these strategies, employed with mindfulness and care, enhances the intricate dance of family dynamics, allowing for a symphony of interactions that celebrate the complex beauty of belonging.

MOVING TO A NEW SCHOOL OR CITY

Transitioning to a novel environment, whether for academic pursuits or familial reasons, presents an intricate mosaic of challenges and opportunities. Amid this shift, fostering a mindset that views this change not as a daunting upheaval but as a fertile ground for personal evolution and novel experiences is pivotal. The initial step in this metamorphosis involves a deliberate mental reframing, where apprehensions are acknowledged yet not allowed to overshadow the potential for discovery and growth that new environments invariably offer.

Finding one's tribe in this unfamiliar landscape necessitates an active engagement with the community, a venture that begins with a mapping of local groups and activities aligned with one's interests. This exploration, akin to sifting through the layers of a new culture to find gems of commonality, relies on both digital platforms and physical bulletin boards, where clubs, gatherings, and community events are often advertised. The act of reaching out, attending meetings, or participating in local activities serves as a bridge, connecting the individual to the fabric of the community through shared passions and pursuits. This integration is a gradual process, requiring patience and persistence, as genuine connections are nurtured over time through shared experiences and mutual understanding.

Adaptation to the prevailing social norms and cultural nuances of the new setting forms the next layer of this transition. Each community, whether a school or a city, operates within a unique set of unwritten rules and cultural codes. Acclimatizing oneself to these subtleties involves a keen observation of social interactions, an openness to learning, and, at times, a willingness to unlearn previously held norms. It is through this adaptive process that one becomes not just a spectator but an active participant in the social life of the new environment, navigating its complexities with an informed sensitivity. This adaptation does not necessitate a loss of one's previous identity but rather an expansion of it, accommodating new perspectives and practices without erasing the essence of one's cultural and personal background.

In the midst of forging new connections, the maintenance of relationships with friends and family from one's previous locale occupies a place of equal importance. The digital age facilitates this continuity through various platforms that allow for regular communication, sharing of experiences, and even virtual participation in significant events. These sustained interactions serve as a lifeline, anchoring the individual to their roots while they explore new branches of their journey. However, this digital bridge requires careful tending, as time differences and life's demands can lead to a gradual drift. Scheduled calls, shared digital experiences, and periodic visits help in nurturing these long-distance relationships, ensuring they remain vibrant and enduring despite the physical distance.

As the narrative of this transition unfolds, it becomes evident that the move to a new school or city is not merely a change of location but a multifaceted process of personal development. The cultivation of a positive outlook transforms potential anxieties into anticipation for new beginnings. The quest to find and integrate into a community resonates with the universal desire for belonging and connection. Adapting to new social norms represents a commitment to cultural fluency, a skill increasingly valuable in our interconnected world. Finally, maintaining ties with one's former community underscores the enduring nature of genuine relationships, transcending geographical boundaries.

In navigating these waters, one discovers that each step, each challenge encountered, and each connection forged contributes to a richer understanding of oneself and the world. This journey, marked by growth, adaptation, and continuity, lays the groundwork for thriving in new environments, equipped with the resilience, openness, and social dexterity that future chapters of life demand.

CHAPTER 9: BUILDING A PERSONAL BLUEPRINT FOR SOCIAL SUCCESS

In the tapestry of life, setting goals is akin to sketching a map for an expedition into unknown territories. Without this map, one might find themselves wandering aimlessly, subject to the whims of circumstance and fleeting desires. Yet, with a clear set of goals—markers of progress and signposts of achievement—the path forward becomes imbued with purpose, each step a stride towards personal growth and social mastery. This chapter delves into the fabric of goal setting, weaving together threads of ambition and pragmatism to craft a robust framework for social development.

SETTING SOCIAL GOALS: SHORT AND LONG TERM

Identifying Priorities

At the heart of effective goal setting lies the act of pinpointing priorities, a process that demands both introspection and honesty. Consider the scenario of wanting to improve conversation skills, a common aspiration. The key is not just to articulate this desire but to dissect it, understanding *why* it holds importance. Is it to forge deeper connections, to enhance professional networking, or perhaps to navigate social situations with more confidence? By identifying the *why*, the goal gains specificity, transforming from a vague ambition into a targeted objective.

SMART Goals for Social Skills

The SMART framework—Specific, Measurable, Achievable, Relevant, and Time-bound—offers a scaffold for constructing goals that not only inspire but also withstand the pressures of reality. Applying this framework to social skills, one might set a goal to initiate conversations with two new people each week for a month. This goal is specific (initiating conversations), measurable (two new people weekly), achievable (a realistic number), relevant (enhancing conversational skills), and time-bound (for one month). The clarity and structure provided by the SMART criteria convert aspirations into actionable plans, each goal a stepping stone to greater social competence.

Balancing Aspirations

The equilibrium between ambitious long-term goals and achievable short-term objectives is delicate, a scale that requires constant attention. High aspirations, like becoming a compelling public speaker, fuel motivation and envision a pinnacle of achievement. Yet, without the grounding of short-term objectives —such as joining a local speaking club or practicing speeches in smaller groups—these lofty goals may float out of reach, untethered by the gravity of practicality. Balancing these aims involves setting intermediate milestones that act as checkpoints, ensuring the journey towards the summit is marked by progress and learning.

Adapting Goals Over Time

Flexibility in goal setting is not a concession to failure but a recognition of growth and change. As one traverses the landscape of social development, priorities shift, new challenges emerge, and what once seemed paramount may lose its luster. Revisiting goals periodically allows for this evolution, enabling the adaptation of objectives to align with newfound insights and experiences. In practice, this might mean recalibrating a goal to expand one's social circle when the initial focus was solely on deepening existing relationships, reflecting a broadening of social horizons.

Visual Element: The Social Goal-Setting Planner

A planner, visually structured around the SMART framework, offers a tangible tool for readers to sketch their social goals. Divided into sections for short-term and long-term objectives, this planner incorporates prompts for specificity, measurability, achievability, relevance, and time-bound criteria, guiding the user through the process of crafting well-defined goals. Additional space for periodic reviews encourages the adaptation of goals, ensuring they remain aligned with the user's evolving social landscape.

In the realm of social skills, where progress is often intangible, setting clear, structured goals becomes the compass guiding one's journey. This chapter, with its focus on identifying priorities, applying the SMART framework, balancing aspirations, and adapting goals over time, lays the foundation for a strategic approach to social development. Through the application of these principles, coupled with the use of practical tools like the Social Goal-Setting Planner, readers are equipped to chart a course towards enhanced social interactions, each goal a milestone in the journey towards social success.

TRACKING PROGRESS: TOOLS AND TECHNIQUES

Journaling for Reflection

Pen to paper, fingers to keys, the act of journaling unfolds as a canvas where the hues of daily social exchanges find their imprint, each stroke a testament to triumphs savored and lessons gleaned. Within the pages of a journal, the routine of reflection morphs into an introspective dialogue, a space where the whisper of progress and the echo of setbacks coalesce into a narrative of growth. This practice, rooted in the ancient tradition of chronicling, transcends its historical confines, offering a mirror to the self in the context of social interaction. Through the meticulous recording of encounters, be they fleeting or profound, the journal becomes a repository of moments that, when revisited, reveal patterns and opportunities for calibration. The discipline of daily entry fosters a habit of mindfulness, encouraging an acute awareness of social dynamics and one's role within them. Successes, once noted, transform into wellsprings of confidence, while areas for improvement emerge as clear waypoints on the path to social adeptness.

Digital Tools and Apps

In the digital age, where technology intertwines with the fabric of daily life, tools and applications designed to track personal growth burgeon, offering innovative avenues for capturing progress. These digital companions, ranging from simple habit trackers to complex analytical platforms, serve as conduits for the quantification of social goals and the milestones achieved towards them. With interfaces that encourage regular input and provide visual feedback, they act as both scribe and counselor, recording strides made while illuminating areas ripe for development. Algorithms, tailored to individual preferences and objectives, churn through data, offering insights that might elude the human eye. The integration of these tools into one's routine not only streamlines the tracking process but also embeds a layer of accountability, transforming the nebulous into the tangible. Features such as reminders and motivational prompts act as digital nudges, maintaining momentum even when motivation wanes.

Visual Progress Trackers

The human affinity for the visual manifests in the creation of progress trackers that translate abstract goals and nebulous achievements into concrete, visual forms. Charts that climb and boards adorned with markers of progress harness the power of visualization, transforming the pursuit of social mastery into a gallery of growth. This visual mapping, akin to charting constellations in the night sky, brings order to chaos, offering a visual narrative of one's journey. The act of filling in a chart or adding to a board becomes a ritual of recognition, a moment of acknowledgment for steps taken, however small. These visual artifacts, placed within daily sight, serve as constant reminders of the path walked and the terrain yet to cover, stirring motivation with the mere glance. The creation of these trackers, whether through digital platforms or the tactile pleasure of manual crafts, invites a creative engagement with one's goals, making the process as enriching as the outcomes it aims to capture.

Regular Review Sessions

Time, in its relentless march, carries with it the risk of obfuscation, where goals once vivid fade into the background of daily preoccupations. Instituting regular sessions dedicated to the review of progress acts as an antidote to this gradual erosion, a scheduled pause for reassessment and celebration. These sessions, islands in the stream of time, afford the opportunity to lay bare the landscape of one's social development journey, examining the terrain covered and recalibrating the course as needed. It is within the quiet of these moments that strategies are refined, achievements are celebrated, and the fodder for future growth is discovered. The ritual of review, conducted with honesty and devoid of self-judgment, fosters a culture of continuous improvement, where each cycle of reflection brings one closer to the zenith of their social potential. Whether conducted solo or in the company of a trusted mentor or peer, these sessions stitch the fabric of progress with the thread of perseverance, ensuring that goals remain alive in the crucible of pursuit.

In the meticulous tracking of progress through journaling, the adoption of digital tools, the crafting of visual progress indicators, and the discipline of regular review sessions, the journey towards social mastery is demystified. Each tool, each technique, weaves into the broader narrative of growth, a story punctuated by milestones achieved and lessons learned. Through the diligent application of these practices, the abstract becomes concrete, the invisible visible, and the journey towards social adeptness marked by clarity, purpose, and celebrated achievements.

LEARNING FROM FAILURE: RESILIENCE IN PRACTICE

Reframing Failure

In the labyrinth of social interactions, paths often diverge, leading to outcomes unforeseen, where failure looms not as a specter but as a guidepost. It is within this intricate dance of expectation and reality that the perception of failure undergoes a metamorphosis, shedding its cloak of negativity to reveal the shimmering potential of growth lying beneath. This transformation, rooted in the acknowledgment that setbacks are but waypoints in a broader narrative, imbues each stumble with meaning, rendering them invaluable for their lessons rather than lamentable for their occurrence. To reframe failure is to engage in an alchemical process, transmuting the leaden weight of disappointment into the gold of insight. It is a reorientation of vision that discerns not the shadow of defeat but the light of possibility that each setback casts, illuminating paths previously shrouded in the dusk of oversight.

Through this lens, the fallout from a social misstep, be it a conversation that spiraled into awkward silence or an overture of friendship that met with indifference, transforms into a crucible for learning. Each misadventure, dissected with the scalpel of reflection, yields nuggets of understanding—perhaps the timing was amiss, the approach misaligned with the context, or the read of the social cues imprecise. This analytical approach, tempered with self-compassion, fosters an environment where growth springs from the soil of mishaps, nourished by the wisdom of retrospection.

Stories of Resilience

The tapestry of human endeavor is stitched with tales of resilience, narratives that span the spectrum of experiences, each thread a testament to the indomitable spirit that characterizes our quest for connection. These stories, beacons of inspiration, cast their glow on the path trodden by those who find themselves ensnared in the brambles of social setbacks. Consider the journey of a once-reclusive individual, for whom the prospect of mingling at social gatherings was a source of deep-seated anxiety. Stepping into the arena of social interaction, armed with nothing but a resolve to transcend this barrier, they encountered, as expected, a series of rebuffs and awkward exchanges. Yet, with each encounter, a layer of apprehension shed, revealing a newfound resilience. This stalwart approach, marked by persistence and the willingness to learn from each faltered step, eventually paved the way to a circle of acquaintances that blossomed into meaningful friendships.

Such narratives serve not merely as tales of triumph but as mirrors reflecting the potential within each individual to navigate the complex dance of social interactions with resilience and determination.

Building a Resilience Toolkit

The construction of a resilience toolkit, an arsenal equipped with strategies to fortify the psyche against the inevitable encounters with social setbacks, is a task both critical and empowering. At the heart of this toolkit lies the practice of positive self-talk, a dialogue of encouragement that counters the tide of self-criticism often unleashed by failure. This internal conversation, nurtured by the recognition of one's worth and potential, acts as a bulwark against the erosion of self-esteem, reinforcing the belief in one's ability to grow and adapt. Coupled with this is the art of stress management, techniques that range from the rhythmic cadence of deep breathing exercises to the immersive tranquility of mindfulness meditation. Each method offers a haven from the storm, a sanctuary where the tumult of the mind is quelled, allowing for clarity and perspective to take root.

In this endeavor, the role of visualization emerges as a powerful ally, where the mind's eye conjures images of successful navigation through social landscapes, rehearsals that prime the psyche for actual engagement. This exercise in mental preparation, grounded in the science of neuroplasticity, strengthens the neural pathways associated with social competence, making the imagined increasingly tangible.

Support Networks for Bouncing Back

In the aftermath of setbacks, the embrace of a support network—a constellation of friends, family, and mentors—provides a lifeline, a source of solace and encouragement that mitigates the sting of disappointment. Within this circle of support, the experience of failure is shared, diluting its potency and reframing it as a collective rather than an isolated journey. Friends offer mirrors reflecting the unaltered worth of the individual, family provides the unconditional acceptance that cushions the fall, and mentors impart wisdom, illuminating the lessons veiled by the shadow of failure. This network, woven from the threads of empathy, understanding, and shared humanity, becomes the crucible in which resilience is forged, transforming the solitary endeavor of bouncing back from setbacks into a communal rite of passage. Through this shared pilgrimage, the realization dawns that setbacks, far from being termini, are mere detours on the road to social mastery, each one a chapter in the grand narrative of personal growth and resilience.

SEEKING FEEDBACK: THE ROLE OF MENTORS AND PEERS

In the labyrinthine quest for social adeptness, the echoes of feedback serve as both compass and lodestar, guiding through the fog of uncertainty towards realms of improvement and self-awareness. This pursuit, however, demands more than mere reception of external observations; it calls for an active engagement in soliciting, discerning, and assimilating feedback from those whose perspectives illuminate the shadows of our blind spots. The art of seeking and receiving feedback, thus, becomes a delicate dance of vulnerability and strength, a willing exposure of one's actions to the scrutiny of others paired with the resilience to mold the insights gained into stepping stones for growth.

Constructive Feedback for Growth

The alchemy of transforming feedback into a catalyst for growth begins with the recognition that every interaction, every exchange, harbors potential insights into the nuances of social conduct. To actively seek feedback is to engage in a deliberate inquiry into one's social dynamics, posing questions that unearth the layers of one's interactions, revealing not just the what but the why and how of one's communicative patterns. The reception of this feedback, however, necessitates a mindset that views critique not as an indictment but as a gift, an offering that, though sometimes wrapped in the coarse burlap of blunt honesty, contains within it the seeds of personal evolution. This process of inquiry and reception demands a humility that opens the door to learning and a determination that forges the path towards refinement and sophistication in social engagements.

Choosing the Right Mentors and Peers

Navigating the waters of feedback requires first the assembly of a crew, a selection of mentors and peers whose insights bear the weight of experience, empathy, and honesty. This crew, diverse in its composition, offers a multifaceted view of one's social landscape, each member contributing a unique perspective shaped by their interactions with the seeker of feedback. Mentors, seasoned navigators of social terrains, provide a macroscopic view, their advice rooted in a broader understanding of social dynamics and professional etiquette. Peers, in contrast, offer a microscopic lens, their observations honed in on the day-to-day interactions that define the fabric of one's social existence. The criteria for this selection thus hinge on a balance of trust and respect, a mutual recognition that feedback, even at its most critical, is grounded in a desire for the other's growth and success.

Feedback Sessions

The orchestration of feedback sessions transforms the nebulous concept of growth through critique into a structured dialogue, a forum where observations are shared, dissected, and assimilated. These sessions, approached with an openness that invites honesty and a specificity that seeks actionable insights, foster an environment where feedback transcends the realm of the abstract to become a tangible tool for development. The structure of these sessions mirrors the precision of a well-conducted symphony, each participant clear on their role, each contribution a note that adds depth and dimension to the collective understanding. The focus remains steadfast on the objective—growth in social competence—with each critique or commendation serving as a guidepost, directing towards areas of improvement or reinforcing strengths already displayed.

In this dialogue, respect serves as the bedrock, ensuring that even the most pointed observations are delivered with a consideration that preserves dignity and fosters receptivity. The goal-oriented nature of these exchanges, underscored by the specificity of the feedback sought, ensures that each session yields actionable insights, transforming the raw material of critique into the refined gold of personal development.

Dealing with Criticism

The terrain of criticism, fraught with potential pitfalls, demands navigation with a compass of self-assurance and a map of differentiation between the personal and the actionable. To encounter criticism is to stand at the crossroads of stagnation and growth, the direction chosen reflective of one's approach to the critique received. The separation of personal feelings from the insights embedded within criticism is akin to the distillation of essence from ore, a process that isolates the valuable from the inert. This differentiation, though challenging, is facilitated by a perspective that views critique as a reflection of actions, not of self, a lens that focuses on behavior as mutable rather than inherent.

The grace with which one handles criticism, then, becomes a measure not of the critique's validity but of the individual's capacity for growth. This grace, a blend of acknowledgment and action, entails not just the acceptance of feedback but the commitment to channeling the insights gained into tangible improvements. It is a stance that acknowledges the discomfort that often accompanies critique while embracing the opportunity for growth that lies within this discomfort. Through this process, criticism transforms from a stumbling block into a stepping stone, each piece of feedback a tool that shapes the sculpture of one's evolving social identity.

In the pursuit of social mastery, feedback emerges not as an adversary but as an ally, a mirror that reflects both the flaws and the facets of one's social engagements. This journey towards growth, marked by the active solicitation of feedback, the careful selection of mentors and peers, the structured exchange of insights, and the graceful handling of critique, becomes a pilgrimage of self-discovery. Through this pilgrimage, the landscape of one's social competencies is both mapped and traversed, each step informed by the observations of those who walk alongside, guiding towards a horizon where personal and social potential finds its fullest expression.

CELEBRATING SUCCESSES: RECOGNIZING YOUR GROWTH

In the vast expanse of social development, where each interaction is a brushstroke on the canvas of our evolving selves, the act of acknowledging achievements—those moments of connection, understanding, and breakthrough—becomes a pivotal anchor. It is through this acknowledgment that the fabric of progress is woven, thread by thread, into a tapestry rich with the hues of growth and transformation. Each success, whether it emerges as a whisper in the quiet of a newfound confidence or resounds as a declaration in the mastery of complex social situations, merits recognition. This acknowledgment serves not merely as a pat on the back but as a beacon, illuminating the path trodden and the strides made, infusing the journey with a sense of purpose and direction.

Celebration Rituals

The creation of rituals or traditions to mark successes embeds these achievements in the physical realm, transforming abstract victories into tangible milestones. These rituals might manifest as simple yet profound acts of self-appreciation—a quiet evening spent in contemplation of progress, a special token acquired in recognition of a hurdle overcome, or a journal entry that encapsulates the essence of the achievement. Alternatively, they could take on communal dimensions, shared with those who've witnessed or contributed to the journey—a gathering of close allies, a shared meal where tales of triumph are the main course, or a collaborative reflection on the growth experienced by all. These rituals, personalized to resonate with the individual or the group, act as milestones, imbuing the journey with a rhythm, punctuating the continuum of development with moments of pause, reflection, and joy.

Sharing Successes with Your Network

The act of sharing successes with friends, family, and mentors not only strengthens the bonds of these relationships but also reifies the achievements in the communal consciousness. This sharing, a gesture of opening one's self to the world, invites those who partake in the narrative to bear witness to the transformation, offering them a mirror to their own potential for growth. It is a reciprocal exchange, where the joy of achievement becomes a shared commodity, bolstering not just the confidence of the one who has achieved but also inspiring those in the network to pursue their own paths of development. This communal aspect of celebrating successes forges a network of support and inspiration, where each individual's triumph becomes a collective asset, enriching the social fabric with stories of possibility and accomplishment.

Reflecting on the Transformation

Regular reflection on personal growth shifts the focus from the destination to the odyssey itself, acknowledging that the essence of development lies not in the culmination but in the journey. This reflective practice, a meditative appraisal of the road traveled, offers insights into the nature of the transformation experienced. It is in these moments of quiet introspection that the nuances of change reveal themselves—not just in the milestones reached but in the subtle shifts in perception, in the deepening of empathy, in the broadening of understanding. This reflection, when undertaken regularly, becomes a practice of grounding, a way to anchor oneself in the reality of continuous change, recognizing that each step, each challenge navigated, and each success achieved is but a thread in the larger tapestry of life's unfolding narrative.

As we weave through the fabric of social interactions, where every thread tugs at the heart of our being, altering the weave of our personal tapestry, the importance of pausing to recognize our growth becomes paramount. This recognition, manifested through personal rituals, shared celebrations, and reflective practices, not only honors the achievements made but also solidifies the lessons learned, embedding them in the bedrock of our evolving selves. It reminds us that progress, in all its forms, deserves celebration, that each step forward, no matter how small, is a victory in the quest for social mastery. And as we continue to navigate the intricate dance of human connection, these moments of acknowledgment and celebration serve as reminders of our capacity for growth, resilience, and transformation, propelling us forward into the next chapter of our journey with renewed purpose and confidence.

CHAPTER 10: SUPPORTING THE SOCIAL EXPLORER

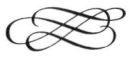

THE CRUCIAL ROLE OF PARENTS AND EDUCATORS

Imagine a tightrope walker, balancing precariously on a slender wire suspended high above the ground. Below, a safety net stretches wide, ready to catch the performer should they falter. This scene, fraught with the tension of potential missteps and the security of support, mirrors the delicate balance parents must navigate in supporting their teens' social development. Here, the tightrope is the burgeoning social life of a teenager, the walker is the teen themselves, navigating the highs and lows of social interactions, and the safety net? That's the parents, providing support without stifling, guiding without controlling. In this critical phase of development, the actions and attitudes of parents lay the groundwork for a teen's social confidence, resilience, and competence.

HOW PARENTS CAN SUPPORT WITHOUT OVERSTEPPING

Guiding vs. Controlling

The line between guiding and controlling is as thin as it is crucial. A parent's role is akin to a lighthouse, providing a beacon of guidance for ships navigating through foggy nights, rather than the captain steering the ship itself. Offering advice on handling social situations, suggesting ways to approach friendships and confrontations, or discussing the nuances of digital communication equips teens with the tools they need. Yet, allowing them the freedom to apply these tools, make their own decisions, and, inevitably, their own mistakes, fosters independence and personal growth.

Open Communication Channels

Envision a garden where communication flows like water, nurturing the seeds of trust and understanding. In this space, teens feel safe to share their victories and defeats, knowing their voices will be heard without judgment. Establishing such an environment requires patience and empathy from parents, who must actively listen and respond with thoughtfulness and care. A regular "check-in" schedule, perhaps during a shared activity or meal, can provide a natural setting for these conversations, ensuring that communication remains a constant, rather than a reactionary measure to challenges.

Modeling Social Behaviors

"Actions speak louder than words" finds profound relevance in the context of social skill development. Teens, ever-observant, absorb the nuances of social interactions through the behaviors exhibited by those around them, especially parents. Demonstrating positive social behaviors—such as active listening, expressing empathy, resolving conflicts calmly, and respecting boundaries—serves as a live tutorial for teens. For instance, a parent resolving a disagreement with a neighbor with composure and respect provides a real-life example of effective communication and conflict resolution.

Resource Provision

In the vast ocean of information, finding resources that resonate with the unique needs of a teen can be daunting. Parents can aid in this exploration by providing books, recommending workshops, or encouraging participation in activities designed to enhance social skills. A curated list of resources, perhaps compiled together with the teen, can serve as a treasure map, guiding them towards valuable knowledge and skills. This could include a mix of classic literature on human behavior, contemporary guides to digital etiquette, or local clubs and groups that focus on public speaking, drama, or other socially enriching activities.

Visual Element: Social Skill Development Plan

A structured plan, visually represented in a chart, outlines a balanced approach to social skill enhancement. This plan delineates specific areas for development, such as conversation starters, empathy building, or digital communication, pairing each with actionable strategies and resources. Regularly revisited and updated, this document acts as a tangible guide for both parents and teens, ensuring that social skill development is approached with intention and attention.

In navigating the complex web of social development, the role of parents oscillates between that of a guide and a supporter, a provider of resources and a model of behavior. Through a balanced approach that emphasizes open communication, leads by example, and equips teens with the tools and resources they need, parents can lay a foundation for their teens to develop into socially adept, confident, and resilient individuals. This chapter, rich with strategies and insights, offers a blueprint for parents to support their teens' social journeys, ensuring that as they walk the tightrope of social interactions, they do so with skill, confidence, and the knowledge that the safety net of parental support is ever-present below.

EDUCATORS AS SOCIAL SKILL COACHES

Within the hallowed walls of educational institutions, a metamorphosis unfolds, one not confined to the intellect but extending its tendrils into the social fabric of the student body. It falls upon educators, those custodians of knowledge and nurturers of potential, to don the mantle of social skill coaches. By weaving the threads of social understanding into the curriculum's tapestry, they cultivate an environment where academic and social growth proceed hand in hand, each enriching the other.

Incorporating Social Skills in Curriculum

In the realm of curriculum development, the integration of social skills training demands both creativity and intentionality. Group projects emerge as fertile ground for this endeavor, each task a microcosm of larger societal interactions. Here, students navigate the complexities of collaboration, communication, and conflict resolution, their roles within the group mirroring those they will encounter in the broader world. Presentations, too, serve as a crucible for the refinement of social abilities, from the articulation of thoughts to the interpretation of audience cues. Peer feedback, when structured to be constructive and empathetic, becomes a tool for mutual growth, teaching the giver as much about compassion and constructive criticism as it teaches the receiver about receptivity and resilience.

Creating a Supportive Classroom Environment

The classroom, in its ideal form, is a crucible for the alchemy of learning, where diverse elements come together to create something greater than the sum of their parts. For this transformation to occur, the atmosphere must be one of mutual respect, collaboration, and empathy. Establishing such an environment begins with the educator, whose behavior sets the tone for student interactions. Respectful dialogue, active listening, and an unwavering commitment to the dignity of each student lay the foundation for a classroom culture that celebrates diversity and fosters a sense of belonging. This ethos, once established, becomes self-perpetuating, as students internalize these values and replicate them in their interactions, creating a feedback loop that reinforces the classroom's role as a safe space for social exploration.

Facilitating Peer Learning

The potential of peer learning is vast, its benefits multifaceted, encompassing academic gains as well as social skill enhancement. By organizing activities that promote learning from one another, educators tap into this potential, creating opportunities for students to mentor and be mentored. This dynamic, when guided by principles of respect and mutual benefit, teaches students about the value of diverse perspectives and the strength found in collective endeavor. Such activities not only bolster understanding of the subject matter but also foster a sense of community and interdependence, as students recognize their roles as both contributors to and beneficiaries of the group's knowledge.

Recognizing and Addressing Social Challenges

Vigilance in recognizing social challenges among students is a critical component of the educator's role as a social skill coach. This vigilance requires an attunement to the subtleties of student behavior and interaction, an ability to read the undercurrents of the classroom dynamic. Training in this area equips educators with the tools necessary to identify issues such as isolation, bullying, or social anxiety, not through intrusive surveillance but through attentive observation. Once identified, these challenges must be addressed with a nuanced understanding of the individual and the situation. Strategies may include individual support, mediation, or the creation of activities designed to integrate and uplift. In each case, the approach is characterized by empathy, respect for the student's autonomy, and a commitment to constructive, rather than punitive, resolution.

In the orchestration of these endeavors, educators act not as imposing figures of authority but as guides and facilitators, their interventions marked by subtlety and sensitivity. They create an environment where social skills are not merely taught but lived, a classroom that mirrors the complexities of the wider social world. Through this holistic approach to education, students emerge not just as scholars but as empathetic, effective communicators, prepared to navigate the nuanced interactions of their personal and professional futures.

CREATING ENVIRONMENTS THAT FOSTER SOCIAL SKILLS

Designing inclusive activities within the realms of both academia and home presents a unique opportunity to nurture the social fabric that binds diverse groups, fostering interactions that transcend conventional social strata. This endeavor, akin to the

CHAPTER 10: SUPPORTING THE SOCIAL EXPLORER | 149

meticulous planning of a garden that welcomes a multitude of species, each contributing to the ecosystem's vibrancy, relies on a deliberate effort to weave activities that cater to varying degrees of social adeptness. Such activities, meticulously orchestrated, not only encourage participation across a wide spectrum but also serve as fertile ground for the cultivation of mutual respect and understanding. In this setting, every interaction becomes a thread in the larger tapestry of community, highlighting the beauty of diversity and the strength found in unity.

The emphasis on diversity and empathy within these shared spaces acts as the cornerstone upon which the architecture of social development is built. It is through this lens that every activity is scrutinized, ensuring that it not only accommodates but celebrates the myriad hues of human experience and emotion. This commitment to diversity goes beyond mere inclusion, venturing into the realm of active celebration, where differences are not just tolerated but revered as sources of strength and learning. Empathy, in this context, emerges not as a byproduct but as a foundational pillar, a skill continuously honed through exposure to and engagement with the broad spectrum of human experiences and perspectives.

The creation of safe spaces where expression is not just allowed but encouraged marks a critical step in the development of social skills. These havens, free from the specter of judgment, offer teens a platform to voice their thoughts, fears, and aspirations, engaging in a process of exploration and discovery that is both personal and collective. In these spaces, vulnerability transforms from a perceived weakness to a shared strength, fostering an environment where risks are taken, failures are de-stigmatized, and growth is celebrated. The act of sharing, in such a setting, becomes an act of courage, each story shared a beacon for those navigating their own social challenges.

Community involvement, extending beyond the confines of structured activities, offers a broader canvas on which teens can paint their social experiences. Engagement in community service and activities not only broadens one's perspective but also instills a sense of belonging and contribution. This outward focus, where the development of social skills is directed towards larger, communal goals, instills a sense of purpose that transcends the individual. Whether through participation in community clean-ups, volunteering at local shelters, or organizing events that bridge generational gaps, teens learn the value of service, witnessing firsthand the impact of their actions on the broader community. This exposure not only enriches their social experience but also embeds within them a sense of responsibility towards the collective, fostering a mindset that values contribution over acquisition.

In this concerted effort to create environments that nurture social skills, the role of deliberate design cannot be overstated. Every activity, every space, every invitation to engage with the community is imbued with the intention to foster connections that are deep, meaningful, and inclusive. It is through this intentional structuring that barriers are broken down, empathy is cultivated, and diversity is celebrated, laying the groundwork for a society that values understanding and cooperation over division and discord.

As we conclude this exploration into the creation of environments conducive to the development of social skills, it's evident that the fabric of our social interactions is woven from threads of diversity, empathy, safety, and community involvement. These principles, when applied with intention and care, not only enrich the social experiences of teens but also contribute to the tapestry of our collective human experience. In fostering environments that celebrate diversity, encourage empathy, provide safe spaces for expression, and promote active community involvement, we lay the foundation for a future marked by understanding, cooperation, and shared growth. As we move forward, let us carry these insights with us, applying them not just in the development of social skills but in all aspects of our interactions, building a world where every individual is valued, every voice is heard, and every contribution is celebrated.

SHARE THE BEAUTY OF SELF-ACCEPTANCE

A powerful connection can start with one small act of kindness. And now that you know exactly how to master all the skills that will empower you to build a healthy social life, you're in the perfect position to help someone who may be struggling.

By simply taking a minute or two to share the skills that resonated with you and the difference this book has made to how you view yourself and the relationships you build, you can help someone feel understood.

TAKE A MOMENT TO SHARE YOUR THOUGHTS!

Thanks for helping me spread the word. Your thoughts can have a butterfly effect, creating ripples of positive change for teens who may be far from you in physical distance, but who understand what you have been through more than you can imagine.

Scan the QR code:

CONCLUSION

As we stand at the threshold of this journey's end, it's essential to cast a glance backward, taking in the landscape we've traversed together. From the initial steps of understanding oneself through the mirror exercise to mastering the ebbs and flows of digital communication, our expedition has been both broad and deeply personal. We've navigated the nuanced art of interacting with others, faced and overcame social challenges, and prepared for life's significant milestones with both anticipation and equipped resilience.

Developing social skills, as we've discovered, is not a destination but a continuous journey marked by patience, practice, and persistence. The path is sprinkled with setbacks, yet, each obstacle encountered is not a dead end but a detour, an opportunity for growth and learning. The strategies we've outlined—be it the reflective mirror exercise, the liberating digital detox, the empathetic approach to relationships, or the empowering visualization techniques—serve as your compass and guide.

The environment surrounding us plays a pivotal role in this journey. Parents and educators, the architects of supportive, understanding, and enriching spaces, have the power to light the way forward with open communication and positive modeling. Their influence is both subtle and profound, shaping the social landscapes we navigate daily.

I urge you, the reader, to leap beyond the pages of this book, to actively engage with the exercises and challenges laid before you. Carve out moments for practice, for reflection, for the deliberate honing of your social skills. This is not a passive undertaking but a vibrant, dynamic process of becoming.

Your social journey is as unique as you are; it is a path marked by individual challenges, victories, and revelations. Embrace this journey, knowing that the pace of progress varies and that each step, no matter how small, is a victory in its own right.

Now, armed with knowledge and strategies, I encourage you to step confidently into the world. Initiate those conversations, join new clubs, navigate digital platforms with intention, and always, always seek to build genuine connections. Let the skills you've honed here spill over into your everyday life, enriching not just your experiences but those of the people around you.

Share your stories of growth, of the obstacles you've faced and the triumphs you've celebrated. Use this book as a conversation starter, as a bridge to connect with others who are navigating their own social landscapes. In sharing, we build a community of support, understanding, and mutual growth.

As we part ways, I leave you with a message of optimism and empowerment. Believe in your ability to navigate the complex social worlds you inhabit, to forge true bonds, to foster resilience, and to make a positive impact on your communities. Remember, the resources listed in this book are but a starting point; the journey of learning and self-improvement extends far beyond its pages.

Together, we've laid the groundwork. Now, the rest of the journey is yours to embark upon. Go forth with confidence, curiosity, and an open heart. The world is richer for your participation in it.

REFERENCES

Introspection and How It Is Used In Psychology Research https://www.verywellmind.com/what-is-introspection-2795252

How to Help Teens Build Emotional Intelligence https://www.newportacademy.com/resources/empowering-teens/teen-emotional-intelligence/

The Effect of Positive Affirmations on Self-Esteem and Well ... https://scholar.dominican.edu/cgi/viewcontent.cgi?article=1010&context=psychology-senior-theses

Fear of judgement: why we are afraid of being judged https://nesslabs.com/fear-of-judgement

Beyond Screen Time: Identity Development in the Digital Age https://www.tandfonline.com/doi/full/10.1080/1047840X.2020.1820214

Preventing Cyberbullying: Top Ten Tips for Teens https://cyberbullying.org/preventing-cyberbullying-top-ten-tips-for-teens

Why a "Digital Detox" Will Benefit Your Overall Mental Health https://www.goodrx.com/health-topic/mental-health/digital-detox

Online Safety (for Teens) | Nemours KidsHealth https://kidshealth.org/en/teens/internet-safety.html

31 Icebreaker Games For Teens For ANY Situation https://www.scienceofpeople.com/icebreakers-for-teens/

How To Read Body Language: Understanding Social Cues https://www.betterhelp.com/advice/body-language/instructions-on-how-to-read-body-language/

Strengthening Your Teen's Social and Conversation Abilities https://www.heysigmund.com/strengthening-teens-social-conversation-abilities/

62 Ways to Politely End a Conversation In ANY Situation https://www.scienceofpeople.com/end-conversation/

40 Empathy Activities & Worksheets for Students & Adults https://positivepsychology.com/kindness-activities-empathy-worksheets/

Ways to Resolve Conflict with a Friend - The Social Skills Center https://socialskillscenter.com/ways-to-resolve-conflict-with-a-friend/

7 Signs Your Teen Is in an Unhealthy Relationship https://www.verywellfamily.com/unhealthy-relationship-signs-in-teens-4065362

Healthy Friendships in Adolescence - CHC Resource Library https://www.chconline.org/resourcelibrary/healthy-friendships-in-adolescence/

7 deep breathing exercises to help you calm anxiety https://www.calm.com/blog/breathing-exercises-for-anxiety

158 | REFERENCES

Rejection Stories Of 9 Highly Successful People That Will ... https://medium.com/@meteor2sky/rejection-stories-of-9-highly-successful-people-that-will-inspire-you-to-succeed-c40d6c200c94

How to Use Visualization for Increased Confidence https://medium.com/lampshade-of-illumination/how-to-use-visualization-for-increased-confidence-techniques-for-creating-mental-images-that-a92a24f507f0

Evidence-based social skills activities (with teaching tips) https://parenting-science.com/social-skills-activities/

Effects of peer pressure on teenagers' mental health. https://mpowerminds.com/blog/Effects-of-peer-pressure-in-teenagers-and-their-mental-health-Find-a-child-psychiatristchild-therapist-near-you

Empowering Teens: Effective Strategies for Teaching ... https://everydayspeech.com/blog-posts/general/empowering-teens-effective-strategies-for-teaching-assertiveness-in-high-school/

Successful anti-bullying program identified by UCLA https://www.universityofcalifornia.edu/news/successful-anti-bullying-program-identified-ucla

Improving Adolescent Mental Health by Promoting Self-Care https://opa.hhs.gov/about/news/e-updates/improving-mental-health-promoting-self-care

Five texting etiquette tips for youth - MSU Extension https://www.canr.msu.edu/news/five_texting_etiquette_tips_for_youth

Social Media and Youth Mental Health https://www.hhs.gov/surgeongeneral/priorities/youth-mental-health/social-media/index.html

10 Digital Miscommunications — and How to Avoid Them https://hbr.org/2020/03/10-digital-miscommunications-and-how-to-avoid-them

The Impact of Video Calls on Relationships and Communication https://cubo.to/blog/the-impact-of-instant-video-calls-on-relationships-and-communication/

Effective communication and teenagers https://parents.au.reachout.com/skills-to-build/connecting-and-communicating/effective-communication-and-teenagers

8 Interview Questions for Teens (With Sample Answers) https://www.indeed.com/career-advice/interviewing/interview-questions-for-teens

Top College Interview Tips https://www.princetonreview.com/college-advice/college-interview-tips

Setting Boundaries For Teens in Dating Relationships https://paradigmtreatment.com/teen-dating-setting-boundaries-for-teens/

How to Help Teens Set Effective Goals (Tips & Templates) https://biglifejournal.com/blogs/blog/guide-effective-goal-setting-teens-template-worksheet

12 Best Goal Tracker Apps for 2024 | Reclaim https://reclaim.ai/blog/goal-tracker-apps

Four Ways Social Support Makes You More Resilient https://greatergood.berkeley.edu/article/item/four_ways_social_support_makes_you_more_resilient

Why Asking For Feedback Can Be A Key To Success https://www.forbes.com/sites/hollycorbett/2022/02/28/why-asking-for-feedback-can-be-a-key-to-success/

Positive Parenting Tips for Healthy Child Development https://www.cdc.gov/ncbddd/childdevelopment/positiveparenting/pdfs/teen-15-17-w-npa.pdf

How to Teach Social Skills in the Classroom [List of Top 12 ... https://pce.sandiego.edu/how-to-teach-social-skills-in-the-classroom-list-of-top-12-social-skills/

The Value of Inclusive Education https://www.opensocietyfoundations.org/explainers/value-inclusive-education

The Benefits of Teen Volunteerism: Transforming Lives and ... https://www.nvfs.org/benefits-of-teen-volunteerism/

Quote Fancy. "Top 50 Oprah Winfrey Quotes." Accessed March 18, 2024. https://quotefancy.com/quote/880081/Oprah-Winfrey-Great-communication-begins-with-connection

Printed in Great Britain
by Amazon